Aircraft Inspection and Maintenance Records

A Practical Guide to Airworthiness for Aircraft Owners, Operators, Pilots and Maintenance Technicians

JEPPESEN
MAINTENANCE
Mastery Realized.

© Jeppesen Sanderson Inc. 2003
All Rights Reserved
55 Inverness Drive East, Englewood, Co 80112-5498

JS312677-003

PREFACE

Aircraft Inspection and Maintenance Records provides practical information for the conduct of aircraft inspections and the completion of aircraft maintenance records. While maintenance, inspections, and maintenance record entries are predominantly the responsibility of Airframe & Powerplant Mechanics, aircraft owners and pilots also must be aware of the scope of various inspections and the maintenance documentation that is required for rendering an aircraft airworthy.

This publication is one in a series of specialized training manuals prepared for aviation personnel.

This series is produced by Jeppesen Sanderson, one of the largest suppliers of aviation training materials in the world. This publication is part of a continuing effort to improve the quality of education for aviation personnel throughout the world.

Specific information on detailed aircraft operations should be obtained from the equipment manufacturer and/or the appropriate regulatory authority through current technical publications, and they should be followed in detail for best results.

This particular manual on *Aircraft Inspection and Maintenance Records* includes a compilation of aircraft inspection and maintenance requirements necessary to meet United States, Federal Aviation Administration (FAA) regulations.

Since some of the words and terms used in this publication may be new to you, this book includes a Glossary that defines all of the highlighted terms.

The validity of any publication such as this is enhanced immeasurably by the cooperation shown Jeppesen by recognized experts in the field, and by the willingness of the various manufacturers and organizations to share their literature and answer countless questions in the preparation of these publications.

For product, service, or sales information, call 1-800-621-JEPP. If you have comments or questions, or if you need explanations about any Jeppesen Aviation Training System, we are prepared to offer assistance at any time. If your dealer does not have a Jeppesen catalog, please request one and we will promptly send it to you by calling the above telephone number, or writing:

    Marketing Manager, Training Products
    Jeppesen Sanderson, Inc.
    55 Inverness Drive East
    Englewood, CO 80112-5498

Please direct inquiries from Europe, Africa, and the Middle East to:

    Jeppesen & Co., GmbH
    Frankfurter Strasse 233
    63263 Neu-Isenburg, Germany
    Tel: 011-49-6102-5070
    Fax: 011-49-6102-507-999

INTRODUCTION

Federal regulations mandate that airworthiness inspections must be completed at specific intervals to verify that an aircraft remains in a legal and safe condition. Generally, these inspections are relegated to aircraft maintenance technicians to perform, but it is the responsibility of the aircraft owner or operator to verify that they are conducted at the appropriate times and that the maintenance records are updated. It is also the owner or operator's responsibility to have all discrepancies repaired or properly deferred until the next required inspection. If maintenance is deferred, the owner or operator is required to verify that maintenance records indicate the conditions that must be met to continue operating the aircraft.

During early development of aviation, the recording of aircraft maintenance was relatively simple, and to some degree, ignored. Within the past few decades, however, improper maintenance record keeping has become one of the most widely pursued enforcement activities within the Federal Aviation Administration (FAA). The reason for the change in attitude is simple—maintenance records are vital to show that an aircraft has been properly maintained in a safe, airworthy condition. Although this is certainly an important consideration, proper maintenance documentation is important for other reasons too. For example, the value and sales marketability of an aircraft is largely influenced by the quality of the maintenance performed. Although the aircraft may be mechanically sound and appear to be in excellent condition, it is difficult to verify the true value of the aircraft without proper historical records. Many owners have had to accept a lower resale price for their aircraft simply because maintenance records were not properly documented or they had been lost.

Maintenance records are also vital for assessing liability once an aircraft has been involved in an incident or accident. This fact may cause some aviation personnel to shy away from documenting the maintenance work they perform in fear of reprisal if a malfunction occurs. It should be remembered, however, that once an aircraft has been released for return-to-service after maintenance, it is the aircraft owner or operator's responsibility to ensure that the aircraft remains in an airworthy condition before and during each flight. Therefore, an accident or incident investigation conducted by authorities involves the scrutiny of all parties responsible for airworthiness. These persons include, but are not limited to, the pilot, the owner, and any individual that has performed maintenance on the aircraft.

It is the intent of this publication to give guidance to all aviation personnel involved in the up-keep of aircraft by highlighting their responsibilities for ensuring safety, legality, and the overall quality of an aircraft. Since an Airframe & Powerplant Mechanic (A&P) generally conducts the required inspections and other maintenance, this book is primarily written to address their responsibilities. Aircraft owners and operators, however, should also be aware of the A&P's responsibilities since the owner or operator is primarily responsible for overseeing the work to determine that it has been completed properly, including verifying that the maintenance actions have been appropriately recorded in the aircraft's maintenance logs.

The requirements for the up-keep and methods of recording maintenance are contained in numerous FAA documents including Title 14 of the Code of Federal Regulations (CFR) and several Advisory Circulars. Many of these documents are reprinted in the appendices of this manual. Additional references are available on-line at the FAA's Web site at www.FAA.gov. The terminology used in the reference publications is often complicated and difficult to interpret, with few standard formats used to document maintenance. This often makes it difficult for aviation personnel to determine what maintenance has been performed to assure that the aircraft meets airworthiness requirements.

Aircraft Inspection and Maintenance Records is designed to provide a clear and understandable foundation in the basics of aircraft inspections and maintenance record keeping. The first part of this text describes the inspection of aircraft, from the types of inspections to the detailed procedures required to perform them. The maintenance record sections describe the responsibilities of the aircraft owner and maintenance technician in the execution and retention of the required maintenance log entries.

At the end of each section, you will find a number of review questions to help your understanding of the material. The answers to these questions are found at the end of the text, along with a final examination so you can check your understanding of the entire publication.

CONTENTS

Aircraft Inspection & Maintenance Records

Chapter 1	Aviation Personnel Maintenance Responsibilities
Chapter 2	Inspections Required on Certificated Aircraft
Chapter 3	Inspection and Maintenance Documents
Chapter 4	Inspection Standards and Procedures
Chapter 5	Performing Airworthiness Inspections
Chapter 6	Major Repairs and Alterations
Chapter 7	Maintenance Records
Chapter 8	Maintenance Record Content and Entries
Chapter 9	Pilot-In-Command Airworthiness Checks
Appendix A	Airworthiness Checklist
Appendix B	14 CFR Part 43 — Maintenance Record Entries (Excerpt)
Appendix C	14 CFR Part 43, Appendix D — Inspection Items
Appendix D	14 CFR Part 91.409 — Inspections
Appendix E	Advisory Circular 43.9C — Maintenance Records
Appendix F	Advisory Circular 43.9-1E — Form 337 Completion
Appendix G	Advisory Circular 39-7C — Airworthiness Directives
Appendix H	Advisory Circular 20-109A — Service Difficulty Program (General Aviation) (Excerpt)

Glossary

Answers to Study Questions

Final Examination

Answers to Final Examination

Chapter 1

Aviation Personnel Maintenance Responsibilities

INTRODUCTION
Aircraft inspections and other maintenance tasks are the responsibility of various aviation personnel. These personnel may include aircraft mechanics, aircraft owners, or even the pilot-in-command (PIC). They also may include employees of a repair station, overhaul facility, or other entity.

Although aircraft mechanics are primarily responsible for conducting maintenance, the aircraft owners and operators also share maintenance related tasks. Each person performs specific tasks to ensure that an aircraft is maintained in an airworthy condition. As aviation professionals, it is important to understand the responsibilities of each person or entity.

AIRCRAFT OWNER
The aircraft owner is the person or organization identified on the Federal Aviation Administration (FAA) AC Form 8050-3, Certificate of Aircraft Registration. The registered owner may be an individual, a group of people (partnership), or a corporation. The owner must be a citizen of the United States, or when registered as a corporation, the corporation must have been created or organized under the laws of the United States or of any state, territory, or possession of the United States.

An aircraft may also be registered as an aircraft of the federal government, state, territory, or possession of the United States, the District of Columbia, or a political subdivision thereof. Other registration regulations are contained in 14 CFR Part 47—Aircraft Registration. [Figure 1-1]

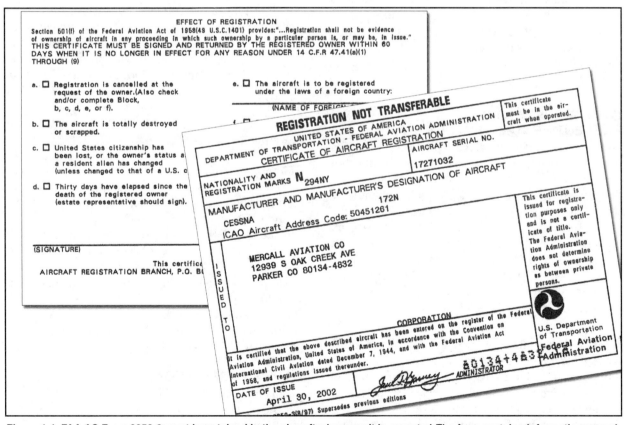

Figure 1-1. FAA AC Form 8050-3 must be retained in the aircraft whenever it is operated. The form contains information regarding the aircraft make, model, serial number, and the name and address of the registered owner. When the owner's address changes, the FAA must be notified in order to maintain an accurate database. This database enables them to notify owners of potential problems regarding safety of flight issues pertaining to their aircraft. Also, when ownership changes, AC Form 8050-3 must be signed by the former owner, or a legal representative, and returned to the FAA Aircraft Registration Branch in Oklahoma City, Oklahoma. Instructions and the mailing address are provided on the back of the form.

1-1

Owners are responsible for determining that their aircraft are properly maintained in an airworthy condition between inspection intervals. This includes repairing the aircraft when a discrepancy becomes apparent, or properly deferring maintenance on a defective item. In addition, it is the owner's responsibility to retain the aircraft maintenance records in a manner that provides clear and concise information with regard to the airworthiness status of the aircraft. They must also provide the appropriate records to a new owner whenever ownership is transferred.

AIRCRAFT OPERATOR

The aircraft operator is the person or organization with operational control of the aircraft. This includes the pilot-in-command for a particular flight, or any person or organization that uses, causes to use, or authorizes the use of the aircraft. For example, if a person rents an aircraft from a flying club, the renter assumes operational control of the aircraft. If the renter is not the pilot, both the person renting the aircraft and the pilot are considered to be an operator.

The operator shares responsibility with the owner in determining whether the aircraft is airworthy as well as verifying that any defects are repaired or properly deferred between required inspections. The PIC, however, is the final authority for determining if the aircraft is in a safe condition for flight. For instance, if a malfunction occurs during flight, it is the PIC's responsibility to determine what action must be taken to satisfy safety and regulatory requirements.

OWNER/OPERATOR PREVENTIVE MAINTENANCE

Owners or operators that hold a pilot certificate may perform preventive maintenance on an aircraft they own or operate. Items that constitute preventive maintenance are listed in 14 CFR Part 43, Appendix A, a copy of which is provided in figure 1-2 (on pages 1-3 and 1-4). When the owner or operator performs preventive maintenance, it is his or her responsibility to properly record the activity in the aircraft maintenance records. The requirements for recording preventive maintenance are further discussed in Chapter 8—Maintenance Record Content and Entries.

AIRFRAME AND POWERPLANT MECHANIC

An Airframe and Powerplant Mechanic (A&P) is an individual certified by the FAA to perform maintenance on an entire aircraft, or one who is limited to perform maintenance on either only the airframe, or only the powerplant. In recent years, it has become common for an aircraft mechanic also to be referred to as an Aviation Maintenance Technician (AMT). Generally, this title is considered synonymous with a mechanic who holds both airframe and powerplant ratings.

A&P MECHANIC CERTIFICATION

When maintenance work is contracted, the aircraft owner or operator should ensure that the mechanic is properly certified and qualified to perform the work. A person holding a mechanic's certificate with only an airframe rating is eligible to perform maintenance on the airframe or any component incidental to the operation of the airframe. They are, however, prohibited from maintaining any portion of the engine (powerplant). For instance, an airframe mechanic can perform maintenance on an alternator or generator, even though these components are generally attached to the engine. On the other hand, a person holding a powerplant rating is limited to maintaining only the engine, its associated components, and propellers.

Occasionally this requirement produces conflicting opinions when assessing if a mechanic is qualified to work on a particular part of an aircraft. For example, consider the following question: Is an aircraft mechanic that holds only a powerplant rating permitted to work on an aircraft exhaust muffler? While it may initially seem that the muffler is a powerplant component, this is not necessarily the case. In fact, most exhaust muffler maintenance instructions are contained in the airframe manufacturer's maintenance manuals. This makes better sense when you consider that the airframe manufacturer builds the exhaust system to meet the specific requirements for the airframe design. For this situation, however, it is generally accepted that either an airframe or powerplant rated mechanic may work on the muffler. This is allowed because the muffler often includes a cabin heater, which is considered to be an airframe system, while the muffler also certainly is associated with powerplant functions.

In another example, an engine-driven fuel pump is considered to be part of the powerplant, whereas an auxiliary boost pump is generally considered to be an airframe component. From these examples you can see that defining specific parts of an aircraft as being related to either the airframe or powerplant can sometimes be difficult to ascertain. To avoid a possible violation of regulations, it's advisable for maintenance work to be done by a mechanic that holds both an airframe and powerplant rating unless the work can be easily discerned as being either an airframe or powerplant related component. [Figure 1-3]

A&P AUTHORIZATIONS

Mechanic authorizations are addressed in 14 CFR Part 65, Subpart D. The maintenance tasks that an A&P is authorized to perform and approve for return to service includes the following items.

- Preventive maintenance
- Minor repairs

APPENDIX A — MAJOR ALTERATIONS, MAJOR REPAIRS, AND PREVENTIVE MAINTENANCE

(a) *Major alterations* —
  (1) *Airframe major alterations.* Alterations of the following parts and alterations of the following types, when not listed in the aircraft specifications issued by the FAA, are airframe major alterations:
  (i) Wings.
  (ii) Tail surfaces.
  (iii) Fuselage.
  (iv) Engine mounts.
  (v) Control system.
  (vi) Landing gear.
  (vii) Hull or floats.
  (viii) Elements of an airframe including spars, ribs, fittings, shock absorbers, bracing, cowling, fairings, and balance weights.
  (ix) Hydraulic and electrical actuating system of components.
  (x) Rotor blades.
  (xi) Changes to the empty weight or empty balance which result in an increase in the maximum certificated weight or center of gravity limits of the aircraft.
  (xii) Changes to the basic design of the fuel, oil, cooling, heating, cabin pressurization, electrical, hydraulic, deicing, or exhaust systems.
  (xiii) Changes to the wing or to fixed or movable control surfaces which affect flutter and vibration characteristics.

  (2) *Powerplant major alterations.* The following alterations of a powerplant when not listed in the engine specifications issued by the FAA, are powerplant major alterations.
  (i) Conversion of an aircraft engine from one approved model to another, involving any changes in compression ratio, propeller reduction gear, impeller gear ratios or the substitution of major engine parts which requires extensive rework and testing of the engine.
  (ii) Changes to the engine by replacing aircraft engine structural parts with parts not supplied by the original manufacturer or parts not specifically approved by the Administrator.
  (iii) Installation of an accessory which is not approved for the engine.
  (iv) Removal of accessories that are listed as required equipment on the aircraft or engine specification.
  (v) Installation of structural parts other than the type of parts approved for the installation.
  (vi) Conversions of any sort for the purpose of using fuel of a rating or grade other than that listed in the engine specifications.

  (3) *Propeller major alterations.* The following alterations of a propeller when not authorized in the propeller specifications issued by the FAA are propeller major alterations:
  (i) Changes in blade design.
  (ii) Changes in hub design.
  (iii) Changes in the governor or control design.
  (iv) Installation of a propeller governor or feathering system.
  (v) Installation of propeller de-icing system.
  (vi) Installation of parts not approved for the propeller.

  (4) *Appliance major alterations.* Alterations of the basic design not made in accordance with recommendations of the appliance manufacturer or in accordance with an FAA Airworthiness Directive are appliance major alterations. In addition, changes in the basic design of radio communication and navigation equipment approved under type certification or a Technical Standard Order that have an effect on frequency stability, noise level, sensitivity, selectivity, distortion, spurious radiation, AVC characteristics, or ability to meet environmental test conditions and other changes that have an effect on the performance of the equipment are also major alterations.

(b) *Major repairs* —
  (1) *Airframe major repairs.* Repairs to the following parts of an airframe and repairs of the following types, involving the strengthening, reinforcing, splicing, and manufacturing of primary structural members or their replacement, when replacement is by fabrication such as riveting or welding, are airframe major repairs.
  (i) Box beams.
  (ii) Monocoque or semimonocoque wings or control surfaces.
  (iii) Wing stringers or chord members.
  (iv) Spars.
  (v) Spar flanges.
  (vi) Members of truss-type beams.
  (vii) Thin sheet webs of beams.
  (viii) Keel and chine members of boat hulls or floats.
  (ix) Corrugated sheet compression members which act as flange material of wings or tail surfaces.
  (x) Wing main ribs and compression members.
  (xi) Wing or tail surface brace struts.
  (xii) Engine mounts.
  (xiii) Fuselage longerons.
  (xiv) Members of the side truss, horizontal truss, or bulkheads.
  (xv) Main seat support braces and brackets.
  (xvi) Landing gear brace struts.
  (xvii) Axles.
  (xviii) Wheels.
  (xix) Skis, and ski pedestals.
  (xx) Parts of the control system such as control columns, pedals, shafts, brackets, or horns.
  (xxi) Repairs involving the substitution of material.
  (xxii) The repair of damaged areas in metal or plywood stressed covering exceeding six inches in any direction.
  (xxiii) The repair of portions of skin sheets by making additional seams.
  (xxiv) The splicing of skin sheets.
  (xxv) The repair of three or more adjacent wing or control surface ribs or the leading edge of wings and control surfaces, between such adjacent ribs.
  (xxvi) Repair of fabric covering involving an area greater than that required to repair two adjacent ribs.
  (xxvii) Replacement of fabric on fabric covered parts such as wings, fuselages, stabilizers, and control surfaces.
  (xxviii) Repairing, including rebottoming, of removable or integral fuel tanks and oil tanks.

  (2) *Powerplant major repairs.* Repairs of the following parts of an engine and repairs of the following types, are powerplant major repairs:
  (i) Separation or disassembly of a crankcase or crankshaft of a reciprocating engine equipped with an integral supercharger.
  (ii) Separation or disassembly of a crankcase or crankshaft of a reciprocating engine equipped with other than spurtype propeller reduction gearing.
  (iii) Special repairs to structural engine parts by welding, plating, metalizing, or other methods.

  (3) *Propeller major repairs.* Repairs of the following types to a propeller are propeller major repairs:
  (i) Any repairs to, or straightening of steel blades.
  (ii) Repairing or machining of steel hubs.
  (iii) Shortening of blades.
  (iv) Retipping of wood propellers.
  (v) Replacement of outer laminations on fixed pitch wood propellers.
  (vi) Repairing elongated bolt holes in the hub of fixed pitch wood propellers.

Figure 1-2. 14 CFR Part 1—Definitions and Abbreviations, defines preventive maintenance as being simple or minor preservation operations or the replacement of small standard parts not involving complex assembly operations.

- (vii) Inlay work on wood blades.
- (viii) Repairs to composition blades.
- (ix) Replacement of tip fabric.
- (x) Replacement of plastic covering.
- (xi) Repair of propeller governors.
- (xii) Overhaul of controllable pitch propellers.
- (xiii) Repairs to deep dents, cuts, scars, nicks, etc., and straightening of aluminum blades.
- (xiv) The repair or replacement of internal elements of blades.

(4) Appliance major repairs. Repairs of the following types to appliances are appliance major repairs:
- (i) Calibration and repair of instruments.
- (ii) Calibration of radio equipment.
- (iii) Rewinding the field coil of an electrical accessory.
- (iv) Complete disassembly of complex hydraulic power valves.
- (v) Overhaul of pressure type carburetors and pressure type fuel, oil and hydraulic pumps.

(c) *Preventive maintenance.* Preventive maintenance is limited to the following work, provided it does not involve complex assembly operations:
(1) Removal, installation, and repair of landing gear tires.
(2) Replacing elastic shock absorber cords on landing gear.
(3) Servicing landing gear shock struts by adding oil, air, or both.
(4) Servicing landing gear wheel bearings, such as cleaning and greasing.
(5) Replacing defective safety wiring or cotter keys.
(6) Lubrication not requiring disassembly other than removal of nonstructural items such as cover plates, cowlings, and fairings.
(7) Making simple fabric patches not requiring rib stitching or the removal of structural parts or control surfaces. In the case of balloons, the making of small fabric repairs to envelopes (as defined in, and in accordance with, the balloon manufacturers' instructions) not requiring load tape repair or replacement.
(8) Replenishing hydraulic fluid in the hydraulic reservoir.
(9) Refinishing decorative coating of fuselage, balloon baskets, wings tail group surfaces (excluding balanced control surfaces), fairings, cowlings, landing gear, cabin, or cockpit interior when removal or disassembly of any primary structure or operating system is not required.
(10) Applying preservative or protective material to components where no disassembly of any primary structure or operating system is involved and where such coating is not prohibited or is not contrary to good practices.
(11) Repairing upholstery and decorative furnishings of the cabin, cockpit, or balloon basket interior when the repairing does not require disassembly of any primary structure or operating system or interfere with an operating system or affect the primary structure of the aircraft.
(12) Making small simple repairs to fairings, nonstructural cover plates, cowlings, and small patches and reinforcements not changing the contour so as to interfere with proper air flow.
(13) Replacing side windows where that work does not interfere with the structure or any operating system such as controls, electrical equipment, etc.
(14) Replacing safety belts.
(15) Replacing seats or seat parts with replacement parts approved for the aircraft, not involving disassembly of any primary structure or operating system.
(16) Trouble shooting and repairing broken circuits in landing light wiring circuits.
(17) Replacing bulbs, reflectors, and lenses of position and landing lights.
(18) Replacing wheels and skis where no weight and balance computation is involved.
(19) Replacing any cowling not requiring removal of the propeller or disconnection of flight controls.
(20) Replacing or cleaning spark plugs and setting of spark plug gap clearance.
(21) Replacing any hose connection except hydraulic connections.
(22) Replacing prefabricated fuel lines.
(23) Cleaning or replacing fuel and oil strainers or filter elements.
(24) Replacing and servicing batteries.
(25) Cleaning of balloon burner pilot and main nozzles in accordance with the balloon manufacturer's instructions.
(26) Replacement or adjustment of nonstructural standard fasteners incidental to operations.
(27) The interchange of balloon baskets and burners on envelopes when the basket or burner is designated as interchangeable in the balloon type certificate data and the baskets and burners are specifically designed for quick removal and installation.
(28) The installations of anti-misfueling devices to reduce the diameter of fuel tank filler openings provided the specific device has been made a part of the aircraft type certificate data by the aircraft manufacturer, the aircraft manufacturer has provided FAA approved instructions for installation of the specific device, and installation does not involve the disassembly of the existing tank filler opening.
(29) Removing, checking, and replacing magnetic chip detectors.
(30) The inspection and maintenance tasks prescribed and specifically identified as preventive maintenance in a primary category aircraft type certificate or supplemental type certificate holder's approved special inspection and preventive maintenance program when accomplished on a primary category aircraft provided:
- (i) They are performed by the holder of at least a private pilot certificate issued under Part 61 who is the registered owner (including co-owners) of the affected aircraft and who holds a certificate of competency for the affected aircraft (1) issued by a school approved under §147.21(e) of this chapter; (2) issued by the holder of the production certificate for that primary category aircraft that has a special training program approved under §21.24 of this subchapter; or (3) issued by another entity that has a course approved by the Administrator; and
- (ii) The inspections and maintenance tasks are performed in accordance with instructions contained by the special inspection and preventive maintenance program approved as part of the aircraft's type design or supplemental type design.

(31) Removing and replacing self-contained, front instrument panel-mounted navigation and communication devices that employ tray-mounted connectors that connect the unit when the unit is installed into the instrument panel, (excluding automatic flight control systems, transponders, and microwave frequency distance measuring equipment (DME)). The approved unit must be designed to be readily and repeatedly removed and replaced, and pertinent instructions must be provided. Prior to the unit's intended use, an operational check must be performed in accordance with the applicable sections of Part 91 of this chapter.
(32) Updating self-contained, front instrument panel-mounted Air Traffic Control (ATC) navigational software data bases (excluding those of automatic flight control systems, transponders, and microwave frequency distance measuring equipment (DME)) provided no disassembly of the unit is required and pertinent instructions are provided. Prior to the unit's intended use, an operational check must be performed in accordance with applicable sections of Part 91 of this chapter.

Figure 1-2. (continued) 14 CFR Part 1

- Minor alterations
- 100-hour inspections
- Phase inspections of a progressive inspection program

Specific details of each of these tasks are covered later in this text.

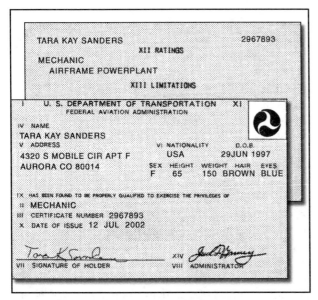

Figure 1-3. Aircraft mechanics are required to have their Mechanic Certificate readily available for inspection by the National Transportation Safety Board (NTSB), FAA, or Federal, State, or local law enforcement officers. Regulations do not require mechanics to have the certificate in their personal possession while working, but it should be readily available for inspection. Although a mechanic is not required to produce the certificate for inspection by other individuals, it's prudent for an owner or operator to verify the mechanic's qualifications before authorizing maintenance work.

A&P technicians may also perform major alterations and repairs, however, they are not authorized to approve the aircraft for return to service after performing these tasks unless they hold an Inspection Authorization (IA) issued by the FAA. Additional IA information is provided in the following section.

Tasks that A&P mechanics are expressly prohibited from performing include any repairs or alterations to instruments, and major repairs or major alterations to propellers. For example, under current regulations an A&P is not authorized to perform maintenance on a magnetic compass (an instrument). In this situation, a mechanic may remove a compass and have it repaired at an appropriately rated instrument repair facility. Once the repair facility approves the compass for return to service, the mechanic may reinstall it and make the appropriate maintenance record entry, including a reference to the name and work done by the facility that conducted the instrument repair. [Figure 1-4.]

Figure 1-4. An A&P mechanic is not authorized to perform repairs to a magnetic compass. This does not, however, preclude the mechanic from removing or installing the instrument. As shown in this photo, the mechanic may also perform adjustments to the compass to compensate for deviation due to magnetic disturbances within the aircraft, commonly referred to as a compass swing.

In accordance with 14 CFR Part 65.81, in addition to possessing the proper certificates and ratings, an aircraft mechanic must also have previously performed the type of work at an earlier date, or must, while performing the work, be supervised by a person that is properly qualified. The regulation is somewhat vague as to the extent that the previous work must have been performed, however. For example, a mechanic who has overhauled a particular make and model carburetor is not necessarily ineligible to work on a different carburetor model. To do the work, however, the technical data and methods used to perform the overhaul must be similar.

14 CFR Part 43.13 also requires the mechanic to use the methods, techniques, and practices prescribed in the current manufacturer's maintenance instructions. Included in this regulation is the requirement that when the manufacturer prescribes the use of special tools, equipment, and test apparatus, the technician must use those items, or an alternate that is acceptable to the FAA. For example, after completion of an engine overhaul, it is common for the manufacturer to require the engine to be test run. When this is done, the instruments used to monitor engine performance must be calibrated to a traceable standard. While an overhaul facility generally possesses these instruments in a test cell or run-up stand, an acceptable alternative for smaller shops or an independent mechanic is to use the aircraft's instrumentation. Before these instruments can be used for performance tests, they must be checked for accuracy, and calibrated by an appropriately rated instrument repair facility. In a similar manner, mechanics should have a method for determining that the special maintenance equipment that they use remains accurate. This includes items such as torque wrenches, precision measuring tools, and pressure gauges.

A&P INSPECTION AUTHORIZATION (IA)

The FAA issues an Inspection Authorization to an A&P once they meet specific experience requirements as detailed in 14 CFR Part 65.91. An IA may perform the following tasks in addition to those allowed an A&P:

- Perform and approve for return to service, annual inspections (except air carrier aircraft)
- Perform or supervise a progressive inspection
- Approve for return to service, aircraft and component parts after major repairs or major alterations when the work is accomplished in accordance with FAA-approved technical data

Specific details of each of these tasks are covered later in this text.

To obtain an IA, an A&P must have been licensed as both an Airframe and Powerplant Mechanic for a total of at least 36 months, and must have been actively engaged in aircraft maintenance for the previous two consecutive years. The mechanic must pass a knowledge exam with a minimum score of 70%. Once the Knowledge exam has been passed, an Airworthiness Inspector from the local Flight Standards District Office (FSDO) must issue FAA Form 8310-5. [Figure 1-5]

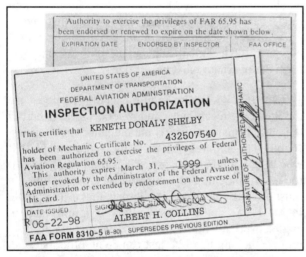

Figure 1-5. FAA Form 8310-5, Inspection Authorization, is issued to a mechanic that meets the requirements of 14 CFR Part 65.91. All inspection authorizations expire on March 31, of each calendar year. Renewal of the authorization is indicated on the back of the form by an endorsement from an FAA Airworthiness Inspector. Renewal requirements are stipulated in 14 CFR Part 65.93.

In accordance with 14 CFR Part 65.95, the IA form is not required to be in the possession of the mechanic while performing IA duties, but must be readily available for inspection at the facility where the work is being performed. The certificate should be available for inspection by an aircraft owner, a mechanic submitting an aircraft, repair, or alteration for approval. In addition, the IA must present their authorization form upon request of the FAA or an authorized representative of the NTSB, or of any Federal, State, or local law enforcement officer.

REPAIR STATIONS

Repair stations are maintenance facilities that have been granted FAA certification to perform repairs or alterations to airframes, engines, propellers, and other component parts of an aircraft. Regulations pertaining to the issuance of repair station certificates are contained in 14 CFR Part 145, which includes a list of the various ratings that a repair station may be certificated for, as shown in figure 1-6.

Before a repair station commences work, the aircraft owner or operator should take reasonable precautions to verify that the facility is properly certificated. A requirement of all repair stations is that they must display their operating certificate so the public can review their FAA authorization(s). If a person is not aware of the authorizations of a particular company, they should ask to see the operating certificate. If there is still doubt as to the authority for the company to do the work, consult an Airworthiness Inspector from the FAA FSDO having jurisdiction over the facility.

REPAIRMEN

The employees of repair stations may be licensed aircraft mechanics, or commonly, many personnel are FAA certified Repairmen. Repairmen are authorized to supervise or perform specific maintenance operations including approval of an aircraft or component for return to service after maintenance, but only for those items that they have been given specific authority for. You should also be aware that a Repairman Certificate is only valid while the person remains employed by the repair station, and only while performing work for the repair station.

Repairmen are also employed by commercial operators and certificated air carriers to perform specific maintenance tasks. In the same manner as repair station repairmen, these personnel are only authorized to perform maintenance functions as described in the organization's Operating Specifications as approved by the FAA. Other repairmen regulations are provided in 14 CFR Part 65, Subpart E–Repairmen.

Repair Station Ratings and Classes

- Airframe ratings
    - Class 1: Composite construction of small aircraft
    - Class 2: Composite construction of large aircraft
    - Class 3: All-metal construction of small aircraft
    - Class 4: All-metal construction of large aircraft

- Powerplant ratings
    - Class 1: Reciprocating engines of 400 horsepower or less
    - Class 2: Reciprocating engines of more than 400 horsepower
    - Class 3: Turbine engines

- Propeller ratings
    - Class 1: Fixed-pitch and ground-adjustable propellers of wood, metal, or composite construction
    - Class 2: Other propellers, by make

- Radio ratings
    - Class 1: Communications equipment
    - Class 2: Navigation equipment
    - Class 3: Radar equipment

- Instrument ratings
    - Class 1: Mechanical instruments (diaphragm, bourdon tube, aneroid, optical or mechanically driven centrifugal instruments)
    - Class 2: Electrical
    - Class 3: Gyroscopic
    - Class 4: Electronic

- Accessory ratings
    - Class 1: Mechanical accessories
    - Class 2: Electrical accessories
    - Class 3: Electronic accessories

Figure 1-6. As shown in this figure, repair station ratings are grouped into classes. Limited ratings are also issued to facilities that are authorized to perform work on specific makes and models of equipment.

STUDY QUESTIONS

1. Under what conditions can an A&P mechanic without an inspection Authorization approve an aircraft for return to service after an annual inspection?

2. Who is the final authority for determining if an aircraft is safe for flight?

3. Can the owner or operator of an aircraft perform preventive maintenance on an aircraft, and if so, what additional requirements must they meet to perform the maintenance?

4. A 100-hour inspection is due at a total aircraft time of 973.3 hours. If the aircraft is enroute between airports when the 100-hour becomes due, can the pilot continue the flight to their destination?

5. True or False. An A&P mechanic is authorized to perform annual inspections after they have held both, an airframe and powerplant rating for at least two years.

6. If a repair station is authorized to make repairs to communications radio equipment, what class and rating must the station hold?

Chapter 2

Inspections Required on Certificated Aircraft

AIRCRAFT AIRWORTHINESS

As previously mentioned, airworthiness is ultimately a shared responsibility between the aircraft owner and operator. To establish airworthiness it is also the responsibility of aircraft mechanics, repairmen, and other personnel to perform their duties thoroughly, ensuring that an aircraft remains safe and legal for flight. Many people that are directly responsible for determining airworthiness, however, do not fully understand what constitutes an airworthy aircraft. In other words, they do not know the standards for airworthiness.

AIRWORTHY DEFINED

In recent years, as evidenced by the number of certificate actions and monetary levies that the FAA has issued for airworthiness infractions, it is apparent that many people involved in determining aircraft condition and legality are not fully aware of the scope of what airworthiness entails. Some feel that airworthy simply means that the aircraft is mechanically safe for flight. While this is certainly one important aspect, it is only a portion of what airworthiness standards encompass.

The term airworthy is not defined in 14 CFR Part 1, therefore many people have been left to interpret the meaning from various other sources. The FAA, however, provides guidance documents that help define the term. In many cases, these guidance documents have been developed through case law studies. For example, an accepted definition of airworthiness can be found in the Airworthiness Inspector's Handbook, Order 8300.10. In accordance with chapter 213, Section 1, Paragraph 5A(2), the FAA considers an aircraft to be airworthy when the following two conditions have been met:

1. The aircraft must conform to its type design. Conformity to type design is attained when the required and proper components are installed and they are consistent with the drawings, specifications, and other data that are part of the type certificate. Conformity includes applicable FAA approved alterations.

2. The aircraft must be in condition for safe operation. This refers to the condition of the aircraft as it relates to wear and deterioration. Such conditions could be skin corrosion, window delamination/crazing, fluid leaks, tire wear, etc.

Analyzing these descriptions further provides the full scope of what constitutes airworthiness.

TYPE DESIGN

When an aircraft, engine, or propeller is initially developed, the manufacturer submits data to the FAA to substantiate that the aircraft or component meets the regulatory requirements for the applicable product set forth in Title 14 of the Code of Federal Regulations. From this information, the FAA establishes a **type design**, which consists of the drawings, specifications, and a listing of those drawings and specifications, necessary to define the configuration and the design features of the product. Once the product is certified, the manufacturer is granted a **Type Certificate**, wherein the type design criteria are published in a **Type Certificate Data Sheet (TCDS)** document. The TCDSs are available on a subscription basis from the Superintendent of Documents, Government Printing Office. [Figure 2-1]

Note that the manufacturers of the airframe, engine, and propeller are each granted a type certificate for their product. In the case of the airframe, the type design includes the allowable engine and propeller combinations that are authorized to be installed on the aircraft, but the specific type design requirements for the engine and propeller are included in their own TCDS. Therefore, when determining that an aircraft meets its type design, it is important to verify that the airframe, engine, and propeller all meet the specifications called out in their respective TCDS.

Type Certificate Data Sheets are further discussed in Chapter III—Inspection and Maintenance Documents.

If an aircraft has been modified in a manner that deviates from its original type design, additional instructions for continued airworthiness must be available. When an aircraft has been modified, these instructions are researched to determine what maintenance actions must be performed to retain airworthiness. For example, an aircraft that was originally type designed for the installation of a particular engine could be altered by the installation of a different horsepower engine that was not specifically approved in the original type design. If this has been done, it would be necessary to determine if the appropriate documentation was available to verify that the engine change was FAA approved, and to determine what other maintenance

2-1

| TYPE CERTIFICATE DATA SHEET |
| NO. 3A12 - REVISION 62 |
| CESSNA |

172	172I
172A	172K
172B	172L
172C	172M
172D	172N
172E	172P
172F (USAF T-41A)	172Q
172G	172R
172H (USAF T-41A)	172S

MAY 15, 1998

This data sheet which is part of Type Certificate No. 3A12 prescribes conditions and limitations under which the product for which the type certificate was issued meets the airworthiness requirements of the Federal Aviation Regulations.

Type Certificate Holder:
Cessna Aircraft Company
P.O. Box 7704
Wichita, Kansas 67277

I - Model 172, 4 PCLM (Normal Category), approved November 4, 1955; 2 PCLM (Utility Category), approved December 14, 1956

Engine Continental O-300-A or O-300-B
* Fuel   80/87 minimum grade aviation gasoline
* Engine limits — For all operations, 2700 rpm (145 hp)
Propeller and propeller limits

1. Propeller
   (a) McCauley 1A170
         Static rpm at maximum permissible throttle setting:
         Not over 2360, not under 2230
         No additional tolerance permitted
         Diameter: not over 76 in., not under 74.5 in.
   (b) Spinner, Dwg. 0550162

2. Propeller
   (a) Sensenich 74DC-0-56
         Static rpm at maximum permissible throttle setting:
         Not over 2430, not under 2300
         No additional tolerance permitted
         Diameter: not over 74 in., not under 72.0 in.
   (b) Spinner, Dwg. 0550162

3. Propeller
   (a) McCauley 1C172/MDM 7652, 53 or 55   30 lb. (-39.0)
         Static rpm at maximum permissible throttle setting:
         Not over 2350, not under 2250
         No additional tolerance permitted
         Diameter: not over 76 in., not under 74.5 in.
   (b) Spinner, Dwg. 0550216

* Airspeed Limits (TIAS) Maneuvering	115 mph (100 knots)
Maximum structural cruising	140 mph (122 knots)
Never exceed	160 mph (139 knots)
Flaps extended	100 mph (87 knots)
C.G. range	Normal (+ 40.8) to (+ 46.4) at 2200 lbs.

Figure 2-1. A TCDS is issued for each certificated make and model aircraft. When differences exist between models, the TCDS contains separate entries for each model. As shown in the upper right-hand corner, the first page of this TCDS shows that it is applicable to each model of the Cessna 172 series airplane.

information is necessary to maintain the aircraft's airworthiness. Additional actions include verifying that the operating limits are correct for the engine and airframe combination and reflected in the form of placards, instrument range marks, and/or aircraft flight manual supplements. Finally, it would be necessary to verify that the aircraft's permanent maintenance records contain a record of the change.

SAFE OPERATING CONDITION

Many aviation personnel enter into the equation when determining if an aircraft is safe for operation. The final authority for determining that an aircraft is safe for flight, however, rests with the pilot-in-command (PIC). The actions that the PIC must perform are numerous, yet each action is vitally important for ascertaining safety. The PIC is also responsible for determining that the aircraft is legal for performing specific kinds of operations. For example, for flight in controlled airspace in instrument meteorological conditions (IMC), the aircraft's altimeter and static system must be inspected each 24 calendar months, yet this action is not required for flights conducted in visual meteorological conditions (VMC). While the aircraft may be airworthy for flight, it may not be legal for all operations. PIC airworthiness responsibilities are provided, in detail, in Chapter 9—Pilot-In-Command Airworthiness Checks.

INSPECTIONS REQUIRED ON CERTIFICATED AIRCRAFT

Aviation maintenance technicians and repair station personnel share the burden of determining when an aircraft is safe for flight by performing airworthiness inspections at specified intervals and repairing, or properly deferring, maintenance discrepancies between inspections. Depending on the type of operation and the operating environment, airworthiness inspections vary in scope, detail and the interval requirements between inspection phases. For example, an aircraft that is used for transporting passengers for hire is required to be inspected more frequently than one that is used for personal transportation. This section details the different types of inspections required on aircraft used in the conduct of various flight operations.

The types of inspections required on an aircraft are determined by the requirements of 14 CFR and several variable factors such as the owners' or operators' type of aircraft, choice of inspection programs, or usage of the aircraft. In most situations, the owner or operator has a choice of several different inspection programs to comply with the airworthiness requirements for their aircraft. [Figure 2-2]

14 CFR PART 91 INSPECTIONS

14 CFR Part 91 contains the general operating and flight rules for aircraft and specifies the inspections

Figure 2-2. The owner or operator of an aircraft is responsible for the airworthiness of their aircraft.

required to determine airworthiness. Subpart E of Part 91 deals with and describes the approved inspection programs for aircraft operations.

Small aircraft are governed by Subpart E and must have a complete annual inspection every 12 calendar months. If the aircraft is operated for compensation or hire, it must have a 100-hour inspection. 100-hour inspections consist of the same scope and detail as an annual inspection, but are performed at 100 operating hour intervals instead of each 12 calendar months. Large and turbine-powered, multi-engine aircraft require more specific detailed inspections that are tailored to their particular flight operations.

ANNUAL INSPECTION

The most common type of inspection required for small general aviation aircraft is the annual inspection. Within every 12 calendar months, the aircraft must have a complete inspection performed to ensure that it meets all the requirements for its airworthiness certification. A calendar month is one that ends at midnight on the last day of the month. For example, if the inspection was completed on January 14, it will remain valid until midnight, January 31, the following year. An aircraft may not be flown beyond the annual due date unless a special flight permit is obtained authorizing the aircraft to be flown to an inspection facility.

The FAA specifies the details of both an annual and a 100-hour inspection in Appendix D of 14 CFR Part 43. This list is not all-inclusive to each aircraft manufactured, but typical of the scope and detail the FAA requires. [Figure 2-3]

The manufacturer of the aircraft generally also produces a checklist in the aircraft service manual that contains at least the minimum items stipulated in Part 43, Appendix D. These checklists, however, are not typically FAA approved sources. Without FAA-

14 CFR - PART 43

Appendix D to Part 43 -- Scope and Detail of Items (as Applicable to the Particular Aircraft) To Be Included in Annual and 100-Hour Inspections

(a) Each person performing an annual or 100-hour inspection shall, before that inspection, remove or open all necessary inspection plates, access doors, fairing, and cowling. He shall thoroughly clean the aircraft and aircraft engine.

(b) Each person performing an annual or 100-hour inspection shall inspect (where applicable) the following components of the fuselage and hull group:

   (1) Fabric and skin -- for deterioration, distortion, other evidence of failure, and defective or insecure attachment of fittings.
   (2) Systems and components -- for improper installation, apparent defects, and unsatisfactory operation.
   (3) Envelope, gas bags, ballast tanks, and related parts -- for poor condition.

(c) Each person performing an annual or 100-hour inspection shall inspect (where applicable) the following components of the cabin and cockpit group:

   (1) Generally -- for uncleanliness and loose equipment that might foul the controls.
   (2) Seats and safety belts -- for poor condition and apparent defects.
   (3) Windows and windshields -- for deterioration and breakage.
   (4) Instruments -- for poor condition, mounting, marking, and (where practicable) improper operation.
   (5) Flight and engine controls -- for improper installation and improper operation.
   (6) Batteries -- for improper installation and improper charge.
   (7) All systems -- for improper installation, poor general condition, apparent and obvious defects, and insecurity of attachment.

(d) Each person performing an annual or 100-hour inspection shall inspect (where applicable) components of the engine and nacelle group as follows:

   (1) Engine section -- for visual evidence of excessive oil, fuel, or hydraulic leaks, and sources of such leaks.
   (2) Studs and nuts -- for improper torquing and obvious defects.
   (3) Internal engine -- for cylinder compression and for metal particles or foreign matter on screens and sump drain plugs. If there is weak cylinder compression, for improper internal condition and improper internal tolerances.
   (4) Engine mount -- for cracks, looseness of mounting, and looseness of engine to mount.
   (5) Flexible vibration dampeners -- for poor condition and deterioration
   (6) Engine controls -- for defects, improper travel, and improper safetying.
   (7) Lines, hoses, and clamps -- for leaks, improper condition and looseness.
   (8) Exhaust stacks -- for cracks, defects, and improper attachment.
   (9) Accessories -- for apparent defects in security of mounting.
   (10) All systems -- for improper installation, poor general condition, defects, and insecure attachment.
   (11) Cowling -- for cracks, and defects.

(e) Each person performing an annual or 100-hour inspection shall inspect (where applicable) the following components of the landing gear group:

   (1) All units -- for poor condition and insecurity of attachment.
   (2) Shock absorbing devices -- for improper oleo fluid level.
   (3) Linkages, trusses, and members -- for undue or excessive wear fatigue, and distortion.
   (4) Retracting and locking mechanism -- for improper operation.
   (5) Hydraulic lines -- for leakage.
   (6) Electrical system -- for chafing and improper operation of switches.
   (7) Wheels -- for cracks, defects, and condition of bearings.
   (8) Tires -- for wear and cuts.
   (9) Brakes -- for improper adjustment.
   (10) Floats and skis -- for insecure attachment and obvious or apparent defects.

(f) Each person performing an annual or 100-hour inspection shall inspect (where applicable) all components of the wing and center section assembly for poor general condition, fabric or skin deterioration, distortion, evidence of failure, and insecurity of attachment.

(g) Each person performing an annual or 100-hour inspection shall inspect (where applicable) all components and systems that make up the complete empennage assembly for poor general condition, fabric or skin deterioration, distortion, evidence of failure, insecure attachment, improper component installation, and improper component operation.

(h) Each person performing an annual or 100-hour inspection shall inspect (where applicable) the following components of the propeller group:

   (1) Propeller assembly -- for cracks, nicks, binds, and oil leakage.
   (2) Bolts -- for improper torquing and lack of safetying.
   (3) Anti-icing devices -- for improper operations and obvious defects.
   (4) Control mechanisms -- for improper operation, insecure mounting, and restricted travel.

(i) Each person performing an annual or 100-hour inspection shall inspect (where applicable) the following components of the radio group:

   (1) Radio and electronic equipment -- for improper installation and insecure mounting.
   (2) Wiring and conduits -- for improper routing, insecure mounting, and obvious defects.
   (3) Bonding and shielding -- for improper installation and poor condition.
   (4) Antenna including trailing antenna -- for poor condition, insecure mounting, and improper operation.

(j) Each person performing an annual or 100-hour inspection shall inspect (where applicable) each installed miscellaneous item that is not otherwise covered by this listing for improper installation and improper operation.

Figure 2-3. As shown here, 14 CFR Part 43 Appendix D contains the scope and detail of 100-hour and annual inspections. Use of this list meets the performance rules for inspections of 14 CFR Part 43.15 (c) (1), which requires the person performing the inspection to use a checklist.

approval, it is up to the inspector to verify that all items addressed in Part 43 Appendix D are included in the manufacturer's checklist. Figure 2-4 (shown in the next four illustrations) shows a sample manufacturer's inspection checklist. The checklist provides the recommended time intervals for items inspected under a progressive, 100-hour and annual inspection program.

PIPER AIRCRAFT CORPORATION
INSPECTION REPORT
THIS FORM MEETS THE REQUIREMENTS OF FAR PART 43

Make: **PIPER NAVAJO** Model: **PA-31 (Turbo) PA-31-300** Serial No. Registration No.

Circle Type of Inspection (SEE NOTE 1, PAGE 3): 50 100 500 1000 Annual

Perform inspection or operation at each of the inspection intervals as indicated by a check (✓)

DESCRIPTION	L	R	50	100	500	1000	Inspector	DESCRIPTION	L	R	50	100	500	1000	Inspector
A. PROPELLER GROUP								17. Check breaker felts for proper lubrication	✓	✓		✓	✓	✓	
1. Inspect spinner and back plate	✓	✓	✓	✓	✓	✓		18. Check distributor blocks for cracks, burned areas or corrosion, and height of contact springs	✓	✓		✓	✓	✓	
2. Inspect blades for nicks and cracks	✓	✓	✓	✓	✓	✓		19. Check magnetos to engine timing (20° BTC)	✓	✓		✓	✓	✓	
3. Check for grease and oil leaks	✓	✓	✓	✓	✓	✓		20. Overhaul or replace magnetos (SEE NOTE 3, PAGE 3)	✓	✓		✓	✓	✓	
4. Lubricate per lubrication chart				✓	✓	✓		21. Remove air cleaner screen and clean	✓	✓	✓	✓	✓	✓	
5. Check spinner mounting brackets	✓	✓		✓	✓	✓		22. Remove and clean fuel injector inlet line screen (Clean injector nozzles as required.) (Clean with acetone only)	✓	✓	✓	✓	✓	✓	
6. Check propeller mounting bolts and torque	✓	✓		✓	✓	✓		23. Check condition of alternate air door and box	✓	✓		✓	✓	✓	
7. Inspect hub parts for cracks and corrosion	✓	✓			✓	✓		24. Check intake seals for leaks and clamps for tightness	✓	✓		✓	✓	✓	
8. Rotate blades and check for tightness in hub pilot tube	✓	✓		✓	✓	✓		25. Inspect condition of flexible fuel lines	✓	✓		✓	✓	✓	
9. Check propeller air pressure (Check at least once a month)	✓	✓		✓	✓	✓		26. Replace flexible fuel lines (SEE NOTE 3)	✓	✓				✓	
10. Check condition of propeller de-icer system Piper Service Manual, Section XIV	✓	✓		✓	✓	✓		27. Check fuel system for leaks	✓	✓		✓	✓	✓	
11. Remove propellers, remove sludge from propeller and crankshaft	✓	✓			✓	✓		28. Check fuel pumps for operation (Engine driven and electric)	✓	✓		✓	✓	✓	
12. Overhaul propeller	✓	✓				✓		29. Overhaul or replace fuel pumps (Engine driven and electric.) (SEE NOTE 3)	✓	✓				✓	
B. ENGINE GROUP								30. Replace hydraulic filter element (Check element for contamination)	✓	✓		✓	✓	✓	
CAUTION: Ground Magneto Primary Circuit before working on engine								31. Check hydraulic pump and gasket for leaks	✓	✓		✓	✓	✓	
1. Remove engine cowl	✓	✓	✓	✓	✓	✓		32. Overhaul or replace hydraulic pump (SEE NOTE 3)	✓	✓				✓	
2. Clean and check cowling for cracks, distortion, and loose or missing fasteners	✓	✓		✓	✓	✓		33. Check pressure pump and lines	✓	✓		✓	✓	✓	
3. Drain oil sump (SEE NOTE 2, PAGE 3)	✓	✓	✓	✓	✓	✓		34. Overhaul or replace pressure pump (SEE NOTE 3)	✓	✓				✓	
4. Clean suction oil strainer at oil change (Check strainer for foreign particles.)	✓	✓	✓	✓	✓	✓		35. Check throttle, alternate air, injector, mixture and propeller governor controls for traveling and operating condition	✓	✓		✓	✓	✓	
5. Change full flow (cartridge type) oil filter element (Check element for foreign particles)	✓	✓	✓	✓	✓	✓		36. Check exhaust stacks and gaskets (Replace gaskets as required)	✓	✓	✓	✓	✓	✓	
6. Check oil temperature sender unit for leaks and security	✓	✓		✓	✓	✓		37. Check breather tube for obstructions and security	✓	✓		✓	✓	✓	
7. Check oil lines and fittings for leaks, security, chafing, dents and cracks	✓	✓		✓	✓	✓		38. Check crankcase for cracks, leaks, and security of seam bolts	✓	✓		✓	✓	✓	
8. Clean and check oil radiator cooling fins	✓	✓		✓	✓	✓		39. Check engine mounts for cracks and loose mounting	✓	✓		✓	✓	✓	
9. Remove and flush oil radiator	✓	✓				✓		40. Check all engine baffles	✓	✓		✓	✓	✓	
10. Fill engine with oil as per lubrication chart	✓	✓	✓	✓	✓	✓		41. Check rubber engine mount bushings for deterioration	✓	✓		✓	✓	✓	
11. Clean engine	✓	✓		✓	✓	✓		42. Check firewall for cracks	✓	✓		✓	✓	✓	
12. Check condition of spark plugs (Clean and adjust gap, .015-.018 as required.)	✓	✓		✓	✓	✓		43. Check firewall seals	✓	✓		✓	✓	✓	
13. Check ignition harnesses and insulator (High tension leakage and continuity.)	✓	✓		✓	✓	✓		44. Check condition and tension of alternator drive belt	✓	✓		✓	✓	✓	
14. Check magneto main points for clearance (Set clearance at .016.)	✓	✓		✓	✓	✓		45. Check condition of alternator and starter	✓	✓		✓	✓	✓	
15. Check magneto retard points for proper retard angle (37° 3')	✓	✓		✓	✓	✓		46. Replace pressure inlet filter	✓	✓		✓	✓	✓	
16. Check magnetos for oil leakage.	✓	✓		✓	✓	✓		47. Replace pressure line filter	✓	✓		✓	✓	✓	
								48. Lubricate all controls (Do not lubricate Teflon liners of control cables)	✓	✓		✓	✓	✓	

Owner:

Figure 2-4. (1 of 4)

Circle Type of Inspection (SEE NOTE 1, PAGE 3) 50 100 500 1000 Annual DESCRIPTION	L	R	50	100	500	1000	Inspector	Perform inspection or operation at each of the inspection intervals as indicated by a check (✓) DESCRIPTION	50	100	500	1000	Inspector
B. ENGINE GROUP (cont.)								18. Check operation - crossfeed valve		✓	✓	✓	
49. Overhaul or replace propeller governor (SEE NOTE 3, PAGE 3)	✓	✓				✓		19. Check operation - emergency shut-off valve		✓	✓	✓	
50. Complete overhaul of engine or replace with factory rebuilt (SEE NOTE 3)	✓	✓				✓		20. Check operation - hater fuel valve		✓	✓	✓	
								21. Check switches to indicators registering fuel tank quantity		✓	✓	✓	
C. TURBOSUPERCHARGER GROUP								22. Check condition of heat ducts		✓	✓	✓	
								23. Check oxygen of heat ducts		✓	✓	✓	
1. Visually inspect system for oil leaks, exhaust system leaks and general condition	✓	✓	✓	✓	✓	✓		24. Check oxygen system operation and components		✓	✓	✓	
2. Inspect the compressor wheel for nicks, cracks, or broken blades	✓	✓		✓	✓	✓		**E. FUSELAGE AND EMPENNAGE GROUP**					
3. Check for excess bearing drag or wheel rubbing against housing	✓	✓		✓	✓	✓		1. Remove inspection plates and panels		✓	✓	✓	
4. Check turbine wheel for broken blades or signs of rubbing	✓	✓		✓	✓	✓		2. Check baggage door latch and hinges		✓	✓	✓	
5. Check rigging of alternate air control	✓	✓		✓	✓	✓		3. Check fluid in brake reservoir (Fill as required)	✓	✓	✓	✓	
6. Check oil inlet and outlet ports in center housing for leaks	✓	✓		✓	✓	✓		4. Check battery, box and cables (Check at least every 30 days. Flush box as required and fill per instruction on box.)	✓	✓	✓	✓	
7. Check turbine heat blanket for conditions and security	✓	✓		✓	✓	✓		5. Check heated for fuel or fume leaks		✓	✓	✓	
8. Check linkage between by-pass valve and actuator	✓	✓		✓	✓	✓		6. Check recommended time for overhaul of heater per Piper Service Manual Section XIII		✓	✓	✓	
9. Inspect induction and exhaust components for worn or damaged areas. loose clamps, cracks and leaks	✓	✓		✓	✓	✓		7. Check electronic installations		✓	✓	✓	
								8. Check bulkhead and stringers for damage		✓	✓	✓	
10. Inspect fuel injection nozzle reference manifold for deteriorate hose loose connections, leaks or obstructions	✓	✓		✓	✓	✓		9. Check antenna mounts and electric wiring		✓	✓	✓	
								10. Check hydraulic power pack fluid level (Fill as required)	✓	✓	✓	✓	
11. Check fluid power lines for leaks and security	✓	✓		✓	✓	✓		11. Check hydraulic power pack and lines for damage and leaks	✓	✓	✓	✓	
12. Inspect for oil leakage from the controller	✓	✓		✓	✓	✓		12. Check fuel lines, valves and gauges for damage and operation		✓	✓	✓	
13. Check operation of compressor by-pass door	✓	✓		✓	✓	✓		13. Check security of all lines		✓	✓	✓	
								14. Check vertical fin and rudder surfaces for damage		✓	✓	✓	
D. CABIN GROUP								15. Check rudder and tab hinges, horns, and attachments for damage and operation		✓	✓	✓	
1. Remove inspection panels				✓	✓	✓		16. Check vertical fin attachments		✓	✓	✓	
2. Inspect cabin entrance, door and windows for damage and operation				✓	✓	✓		17. Check rudder and tab hinge bolts for excess wear		✓	✓	✓	
3. Check emergency exit latching mechanism				✓	✓	✓		18. Check rudder trim measurement		✓	✓	✓	
4. Check upholstery for tears				✓	✓	✓		19. Check horizontal stabilizer and elevator surfaces for damage		✓	✓	✓	
5. Check seats, seat belts, security brackets and bolts				✓	✓	✓		20. Check elevator and tab hinges, horns, and attachments for damage and operation		✓	✓	✓	
6. Check trim operation				✓	✓	✓		21. Check horizontal stabilizer attachments		✓	✓	✓	
7. Check rudder pedals				✓	✓	✓		22. Check elevator and tab hinge bolts and bearings for excess wear		✓	✓	✓	
8. Check parking breaks				✓	✓	✓		23. Check elevator trim mechanism		✓	✓	✓	
9. Check control wheels, column, pulleys and cable				✓	✓	✓		24. Check aileron, rudder, elevator and trim cables, turnbuckles, guides and pulleys for safety, damage and operation		✓	✓	✓	
10. Check landing, navigation, cabin and instrument lights				✓	✓	✓		25. Clean and lubricate elevator and rudder trim drum screw			✓	✓	
11. Check instruments, lines and attachments				✓	✓	✓		26. Check rotating beacon for security and operation		✓	✓	✓	
12. Check gyro operated instruments and electric turn and bank (overhaul or replace as required)				✓	✓	✓		27. Lubricate per lubrication chart		✓	✓	✓	
								28. Check conditions of pneumatic de-icers		✓	✓	✓	
13. Check pilot tubes), lines and static vents for condition, security and stoppage				✓	✓	✓		29. Check security of AutoPilot servo bridle cable clamps		✓	✓	✓	
14. Check altimeter (Calibrate altimeter system in accordance with FAR 91.170, if appropriate)				✓	✓	✓		**F. WING GROUP**					
15. Change manifold pressure gauge filter				✓	✓	✓		1. Remove inspection plates and panels		✓	✓	✓	
16. Diana crossfeed line				✓	✓	✓		2. Check surfaces, sinks and tips for damage and loose rivets		✓	✓	✓	
17. Check operation - fuel selector valve				✓	✓	✓							

Figure 2-4. (2 of 4)

Whereas Part 43 Appendix D is generic to all aircraft, the manufacturer's checklist contains specific information regarding their product, and therefore encompasses additional details. As another alternative, some inspectors may create a checklist of their own design. This is allowed, providing the checklist contains the minimum scope and detail prescribed in Part 43, Appendix D.

Annual inspections must be performed by an A&P technician holding an Inspection Authorization or by an inspector authorized by an appropriately rated

Circle Type of Inspection (SEE NOTE 1, PAGE 3) 50 100 500 1000 Annual DESCRIPTION	50	100	500	1000	Inspector	Perform inspection or operation at each of the inspection intervals as indicated by a check (✓) DESCRIPTION	50	100	500	1000	Inspector
F. WING GROUP (cont.)						17. Check torque link bolts and bushings (Rebush as required)			✓	✓	
3. Check ailerons and tab hinges and attachments		✓	✓	✓		18. Check drag and side brace link bolts (Replace as required)				✓	
4. Check aileron and trim cables, pulleys and bellcranks for damage and operation		✓	✓	✓		19. Check gear doors and attachments		✓	✓	✓	
5. Check aileron balance weight for security		✓	✓	✓		20. Check warning horn and light for operation		✓	✓	✓	
6. Check flaps and attachments for damage and operations		✓	✓	✓		21. Retract gear - check operation		✓	✓	✓	
7. Inspect condition of bolts used with flap and aileron hinges (Replace as required.)				✓		22. Retract gear - check doors for clearance and operation		✓	✓	✓	
8. Check all exterior bearings			✓	✓		23. Check anti-retraction system,		✓	✓	✓	
9. Lubricate per lubrication chart	✓	✓	✓	✓		24. Check actuating cylinders for leaking and security		✓	✓	✓	
10. Check wing attachment bolts and brackets		✓	✓	✓		25. Check position indicating switches and electrical leads for security		✓	✓	✓	
11. Check engine mount attaching structures		✓	✓	✓		26. Lubricate per lubrication chart		✓	✓	✓	
12. Remove, drain, and clean fuel filter bowl and screen (Drain and clean at least every 90 days)	✓	✓	✓	✓		27. Remove airplane from jacks		✓	✓	✓	
13. Check fuel cells and lines for leaks and water		✓	✓	✓		**H. OPERATIONAL INSPECTION**					
14. Fuel tanks marked for capacity		✓	✓	✓		1. Check fuel pump, fuel cell selector and crossfeed operation	✓	✓	✓	✓	
15. Fuel tanks marked for minimum octane rating		✓	✓	✓		2. Check fuel quantity and pressure of flow	✓	✓	✓	✓	
16. Check fuel cell vents		✓	✓	✓		3. Check oil pressure and temperature	✓	✓	✓	✓	
17. Check condition of pneumatic de-icers		✓	✓	✓		4. Check alternator output	✓	✓	✓	✓	
G LANDING GEAR GROUP						5. Check manifold pressure	✓	✓	✓	✓	
1. Check oleo struts for proper extension (Check for proper fluid level as required)	✓	✓	✓	✓		6. Check alternate air	✓	✓	✓	✓	
2. Check nose gear steering control and travel		✓	✓	✓		7. Check parking brake	✓	✓	✓	✓	
3. Check wheels for alignment		✓	✓	✓		8. Check gyro pressure gage	✓	✓	✓	✓	
4. Put airplane on jack		✓	✓	✓		9. Check gyro for noise and roughness	✓	✓	✓	✓	
5. Check tires for cuts, uneven or excessive wear and slippage		✓	✓	✓		10. Check cabin heater operation	✓	✓	✓	✓	
6. Remove wheels, clean, check and repack bearings			✓	✓		11. Check magneto switch operation	✓	✓	✓	✓	
7. Check wheels for cracks, corrosion and broken bolts		✓	✓	✓		12. Check magneto RPM variation	✓	✓	✓	✓	
8. Check tire pressure (N42-M60)	✓	✓	✓	✓		13. Check throttle and mixture operation	✓	✓	✓	✓	
9. Check brake lining and disc		✓	✓	✓		14. Check propeller smoothness	✓	✓	✓	✓	
10. Check brake backing plates		✓	✓	✓		15. Check propeller governor action	✓	✓	✓	✓	
11. Check brake and hydraulic lines		✓	✓	✓		**I. GENERAL**					
12. Check shimmy dampener		✓	✓	✓		1. Aircraft conforms to FAA Specifications	✓	✓	✓	✓	
13. Check gear forks for damage		✓	✓	✓		2. All FAA Airworthiness Directives complied with	✓	✓	✓	✓	
14. Check oleo struts for fluid leaks and scoring		✓	✓	✓		3. All Manufacturers Service Letters and Bulletins complied with	✓	✓	✓	✓	
15. Check gear struts, attachments, torque links, reaction links and bolts for condition and security		✓	✓	✓		4. Check for proper flight manual	✓	✓	✓	✓	
16. Check downlock for operation and adjustment		✓	✓	✓		5. Aircraft papers in proper order	✓	✓	✓	✓	

NOTES:
1. Both the annual and 100 hour inspections are complete inspections of the airplane — identical in scope. Inspections must be accomplished by persons authorized by FAA.
2. Intervals between oil changes can be increased as much as 100% on engines equipped with full flow (carriage type) oil filters — provided the element is replaced each 50 hours of operation.
3. Replace or overhaul as required or at engine overhaul. (For engine overhaul, refer to Lycoming Service Instructions No. 1009.)

REMARKS:

Signature of Mechanic or Inspector	Certificate No.	Date	Total Time on Airplane

Figure 2-4. (3 of 4)

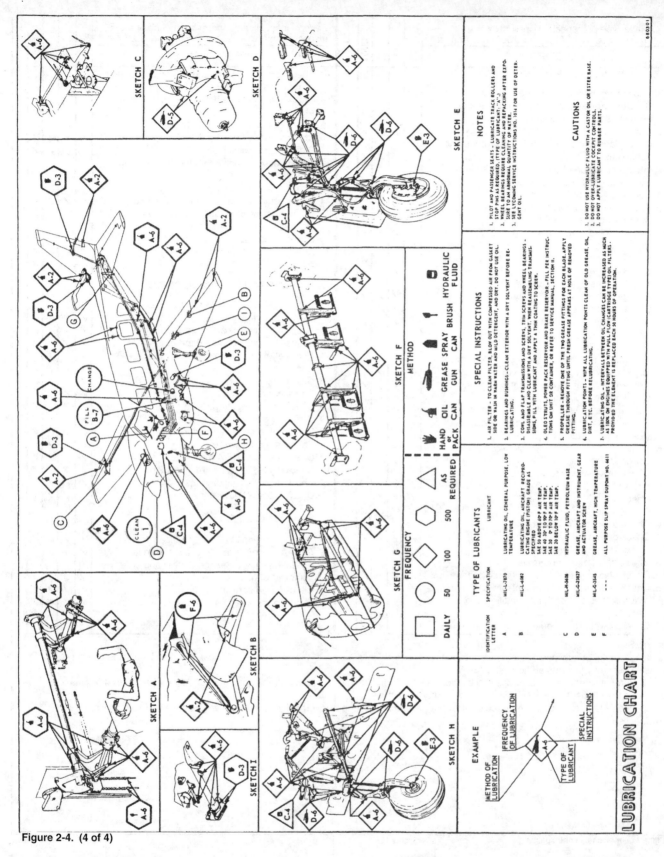

Figure 2-4. (4 of 4)

repair station. If the aircraft passes the inspection, inspectors must write up the inspection results in the maintenance records, and approve the aircraft for return to service. If for any reason the aircraft does not meet airworthiness requirements, the inspector must provide a list of discrepancies and unairworthy items to the aircraft owner. The inspector may not delegate any annual inspection responsibility to another person. However, any certified A&P technician may correct the discrepancies the inspector listed and then approve the aircraft for return to service, as long as the discrepancy found does not require a major repair. In fact, if the repair is an item covered under preventive maintenance, the owner or operator of the aircraft may also perform the repairs and approve the aircraft for return to service. The due date of the next annual inspection is then based on the date of the original inspection and not on the date that the discrepancies were corrected. For example, if an aircraft's annual was completed on March 20, but a discrepancy repair was not completed until April 15, the next annual is still due March 30, the following year.

If the aircraft does not pass the annual inspection, it may not be flown until the unairworthy items are corrected. However, if the owner wants to fly the aircraft to a different repair location, a special flight permit may be obtained to ferry the aircraft.

100-HOUR INSPECTION

If the aircraft is operated for compensation or hire, it must be given a complete inspection containing the same scope and detail as the annual inspection every 100 hours of operation unless it is maintained under an FAA-approved, alternative inspection program such as a progressive inspection. In the case of a 100-hour inspection, the time limitation may be exceeded by no more than 10 hours of flight operating time to reach a location where the inspection can be conducted. The excess time used to reach the inspection location, however, must be included in computing the next 100 hours time in service. For example, if a 100-hour inspection was due at 1000 hours and the aircraft was flown for 4 hours over the time limit to reach the inspection location, the next 100-hour inspection would still be due at 1100 hours time in service.

The difference between a 100-hour and an annual inspection is that a certified A&P technician may conduct the 100-hour inspection and approve the aircraft for return to service. The A&P technician who inspects the aircraft must make the proper entries in the aircraft's maintenance records and approve the aircraft for return to service before the 100-hour inspection is considered complete.

Like the inspector performing an annual, the A&P inspecting the aircraft may not supervise the inspection process. The maintenance technician performing the 100-hour inspection is responsible for approving the aircraft for return to service. In other words, the A&P signing off the aircraft must be the one who actually performs the inspection. However, the inspector may utilize other A&Ps or repairmen in the preparation for the inspection such as removing inspection panels, cowlings, and fairings. In addition, any certified A&P technician may correct and sign-off any discrepancies found by the inspector as long as they are not major repairs or major alterations.

100-hour inspections may be signed off as annual inspections if an A&P mechanic holding an inspection authorization (IA) completed the inspection. In a sense, the aircraft could have several annuals performed in one calendar year at each 100 hours of operation. However, a 100-hour inspection may not take the place of an annual inspection. If an aircraft is operated under the requirements of an annual inspection, it must be inspected by an A&P who holds an IA rating or a certified repair station inspector and signed-off as an annual inspection.

PROGRESSIVE INSPECTION

At times, aircraft operators may feel that it is not economical to keep the airplane out of commission long enough to perform a complete annual inspection at one time. As an alternative, the owner may elect to use a progressive inspection schedule. A progressive inspection is exactly the same in scope and detail as the annual inspection but allows the workload to be divided into smaller portions and performed in shorter time periods. For example, the engine may be inspected at one time, the airframe inspection may be conducted at another time, and components such as the landing gear at another. Progressive inspection schedules must ensure that the aircraft will be airworthy at all times and conform to all applicable FAA aircraft specifications, type certificate data sheets, airworthiness directives, and other required data.

The manufacturer provides guidelines to help an operator select an appropriate inspection program for their specific operation. For example, if an aircraft is flown more than 200 hours per calendar year, a progressive inspection program is most likely recommended to reduce aircraft downtime and overall maintenance costs.

The aircraft inspection table outlining a typical progressive inspection schedule is similar to that shown in figure 2-4. For a progressive inspection schedule, however, there are items inspected at 50, 100, or 200 hours. The inspection intervals are separated in such a way to result in a complete aircraft inspection every 200 flight hours.

Before a progressive inspection schedule may be implemented, the FAA must approve the inspection program. The owner must submit a written request outlining their intended progressive inspection guidelines to the local FSDO for approval. Once approved, and before the progressive inspection program may begin, the aircraft must undergo a complete annual inspection. After the initial complete inspection, routine and detailed inspections must be conducted as prescribed in the progressive inspection schedule. Routine inspections consist of visual and operational checks of the aircraft, engines, appliances, components and systems, without disassembly. Detailed inspections consist of thorough checks of the aircraft, engines, appliances, components and systems including necessary disassembly. The overhaul of a component, engine, or system is considered a detailed inspection.

A progressive inspection program requires that a current and FAA-approved inspection procedure manual for the particular airplane be available to the pilot and maintenance technician. The manual explains the progressive inspection and outlines the required inspection intervals. All items in the inspection schedule must be completed within the 12 calendar months that are allowed for an annual inspection. The progressive inspection differs from the annual or 100-hour inspection in that a certified mechanic holding an inspection authorization, a certified repair station, or the aircraft manufacturer may supervise or conduct the inspection.

If the progressive inspection is discontinued, the owner or operator must immediately notify the local FSDO of the discontinuance. In addition, the first complete inspection is due within 12 calendar months or, in the case of commercial operations, 100 hours of operation from the last complete inspection that was performed under the progressive inspection schedule.

LARGE AND TURBINE-POWERED MULTI-ENGINE AIRCRAFT

Large (over 12,500 lbs. gross takeoff weight) and multi-engine turbine aircraft operating under 14 CFR Part 91, require inspection programs tailored to the specific aircraft and its unique operating conditions. These unique conditions would include scenarios such as high flight times, or aircraft operating in extremely humid environments or in extremely cold climates. Because of the size and complexity of most turbine-powered aircraft, the FAA requires a more detailed and encompassing inspection program to meet the needs of these aircraft and flying conditions. Although they may be operated under Part 91, large and turbine-powered aircraft are often inspected under programs normally utilized by air carrier or air taxi operations.

The registered owner or operator of a large or turbine-powered aircraft operating under Part 91 must select, identify in the aircraft maintenance records, and use one of the following inspection programs: a continuous airworthiness inspection program, an approved aircraft inspection program (AAIP), the manufacturer's current recommended inspection program, or any other inspection program developed by the owner/operator and approved by the FAA. The exception is in the case of turbine-powered rotorcraft operations, in which case, the owner/operator may choose to use the inspection provisions set out for small aircraft: annual, 100-hour, or progressive inspection programs. After selection, the operator must submit an inspection schedule, along with instructions and procedures regarding the performance of the inspections, including all tests and checks, to the local FAA FSDO for approval.

A continuous airworthiness inspection program is designed for commercial operators of large aircraft operating under 14 CFR Parts, 121, 127, or 135. It is one element of an overall continuous airworthiness maintenance program (CAMP) currently being utilized by an air carrier that is operating that particular make and model aircraft. [Figure 2-5]

Figure 2-5. Large turbine-powered corporate jet owners may elect to use a continuous airworthiness inspection program because of the complexity of the aircraft and its systems.

A continuous airworthiness inspection program might be chosen under Part 91 operations when an air carrier purchases or leases an aircraft operating under another air carrier's 121 certificate. For example, Airline B purchases an aircraft from Airline A. The aircraft must be operated under an inspection program during the transition from Airline A to Airline B. Instead of creating an entirely new inspection program tailored to the specific aircraft during this transition period, Airline B may choose to keep the aircraft on its current continuous airworthiness inspection program until it is placed on the new owner's Part 121 operating certificate.

An approved aircraft inspection program (AAIP) may be chosen by on-demand operators who operate under Part 135. If the FAA determines that annual, 100-hour, or progressive inspections are not adequate to meet Part 135 operations, they may require or allow the implementation of an AAIP for any make and model aircraft the operator exclusively uses. The AAIP is similar to the CAMP utilized by most part 121 air carriers. This program encompasses maintenance and inspection into an overall continuous maintenance program. [Figure 2-6]

A complete manufacturer's recommended inspection program consists of the inspection program supplied by the airframe manufacturer and supplemented by the inspection programs provided by the manufacturers of

Figure 2-6. Turbo-prop aircraft are typical of the type operated by air-taxi operators. Each aircraft operated by air-taxi operators may be maintained under an AAIP designed specifically to meet that particular aircraft by registration and serial number.

the engines, propellers, appliances, survival equipment, and emergency equipment installed on the aircraft. A manufacturer's inspection program is used more frequently when an aircraft is factory new. If an aircraft has several modifications, updated systems or custom avionics not installed at the factory, the manufacturer's inspection program alone may not be adequate in the overall inspection of the aircraft and its installed equipment and components. In this case, another method of inspection must be chosen.

The owner of an aircraft may choose to develop their own inspection program. The recommended manufacturer's inspection program is generally used as the basis of an owner developed inspection plan. However, deviation from the manufacturer's inspection program must be supported and approved by the FAA. The customized plan must include the inspection methods, techniques, practices, and standards necessary for the proper completion of the program. Most owner developed inspection programs include inspection and repair requirements only, and do not require continual maintenance to be performed on the aircraft.

CONFORMITY INSPECTIONS

Aircraft are manufactured to FAA approved specifications. Alterations made to the original design specifications of the aircraft require approval in the form of a sign-off from a certificated maintenance technician or, in the case of a major repair or alteration, approval from an appropriate authority on FAA Form 337. The absence of approval for any alteration renders the aircraft unairworthy. A conformity inspection is an essential element of all aircraft inspection programs and performed to determine whether the aircraft conforms to, or matches its approved specifications.

A conformity inspection is essentially a visual inspection that compares the approved aircraft specifications with the actual aircraft and associated engine and components. A list is compiled outlining the information gathered from the Type Certificate Data Sheet (TCDS), applicable Supplemental Type Certificate Data Sheets (STC), major repair & alteration information (FAA Form 337), aircraft equipment list, airworthiness directive compliance record, etc. Specific information regarding each of these items is discussed in chapter 3—Inspection and Maintenance Documents. The list includes model numbers, part numbers, serial numbers, installation dates, overhaul times, and any other pertinent information obtained in the reference documents. The mechanic performs a visual inspection and compares the aircraft with the compiled list of information making note of any deviation from the aircraft specifications.

A conformity inspection is not specifically required by name, but it is inherently required at every inspection interval due to the nature of the inspection. A conformity inspection is performed to determine whether the aircraft conforms to its certification specifications. A conformity inspection is specifically required, however, when an aircraft is exported to or imported from another country. Further, a conformity inspection is highly recommended when performing a pre-purchase inspection for a prospective aircraft buyer.

Although the conformity inspection is an important part of the overall inspection process, it is one of the most common inspection tasks neglected or not completely carried out. For example, many times an IA inspector fails to visually verify the equipment installed on the aircraft with the equipment list. In doing so, the IA may overlook a piece of equipment installed on the aircraft, but not documented in the maintenance records, which could render the aircraft unairworthy. The verification of the presence of equipment installed in the aircraft, but failure to verify that the installation was properly performed may also render the aircraft unairworthy. The inspector must not only verify the physical presence of items but also confirm whether the installation of the equipment was properly performed, especially if the installation of the equipment was done without proper documentation.

A skilled and effective inspector meticulously verifies the installation of equipment list items. Not only verifying that they are physically in the aircraft, but also that they were properly installed and, in the case of major repair or alteration, that a Form 337 was created and approved by the FAA.

AIR CHARTER & AIR CARRIER OPERATIONS

Aircraft operators regulated under 14 CFR Part 121 or 135 must maintain their aircraft under comprehensive maintenance and inspection programs. One of the differences between Part 91 operations and Air Carrier operations is that Part 121 operators must perform scheduled maintenance as well as scheduled inspections on their aircraft.

Ongoing scheduled maintenance is not required on aircraft operated under Part 91. The operating rules of Part 91 only require an owner to correct discrepancies as they occur between or during inspections. Air carriers, on the other hand, must perform aircraft inspections AND scheduled maintenance on a continual basis. This includes many servicing requirements such as lubricating mechanical airframe assemblies, servicing oxygen and fire suppression systems and other similar tasks on an on-going basis.

Air charter operations regulated under Part 135 offer another unique operating environment. Depending on the size and complexity of aircraft operated, a range of inspection rules apply. Part 135 operators may choose from several different inspection programs depending on the number of seats and complexity of the aircraft.

PART 135 AIR CHARTER INSPECTIONS

Part 135 on-demand air charter operators have several different options regarding the type of inspection programs with which they must comply. Air charter companies that operate aircraft with less than 10 passenger seats may choose to inspect these aircraft under 14 CFR Part 91 and Part 43 rules, 100-hour or progressive inspection programs. In other words, they are not required to perform continual scheduled maintenance on their aircraft, only inspections and discrepancy repairs, as required. Air charter operators that operate aircraft with 10 or more passenger seats are required to implement a more-encompassing continual maintenance and inspection program. They may choose to implement an Approved Aircraft Inspection Program (AAIP), a current manufacturer's inspection program, or an operator developed inspection and maintenance program approved by the FAA.

An AAIP is the inspection program most often implemented by 14 CFR Part 135 operators. It is similar to a continuous airworthiness maintenance program used by Part 121 air carriers, described in the following section. However, AAIPs are not fleet inspection programs and do not require continual scheduled maintenance. They require continual scheduled inspections only and are set up for the individual aircraft by registration number and serial number. Air charter operations may have several different AAIPs for different aircraft operated.

For example, an air charter business that operates an aircraft with 9 or fewer passenger seats may inspect that particular aircraft under 100-hour or progressive inspection intervals. The same operation may also operate several larger, complex aircraft and inspect them under separate AAIPs. It is possible for an air charter operator to use a different inspection program for each of its aircraft, such as progressive for one or AAIP for another, etc. [Figure 2-7]

Figure 2-7. Air medical operators may operate several different types of airplanes and helicopters and inspect each under separate inspection programs. AAIPs are not fleet programs; they are inspection programs designed for individual aircraft. A charter company that owns and operates five different aircraft could conceivably operate them under five different AAIPs, each specific to an individual aircraft.

Manufacturer's inspection programs are more specific than the 100-hour or annual inspections but lack the ease and control provided by the approved aircraft inspection program. An AAIP allows the operator to choose their own maintenance and inspection schedules. An AAIP is not considered to be better than a manufacturer's program, however, an AAIP provides the FAA inspector with more control of the program's content. It requires the operator to validate its program's and revisions to the inspector which manufacturer's programs do not. This is not to say that a manufacturer's program cannot be used, but it must be identified as an AAIP and approved for a particular operator as that operator's program, not the manufacturer's.

When establishing an AAIP, it should include avionics, instrument systems, and appliances. These types of systems are not always installed by the aircraft manufacturer and may not be included in their recommended inspection program. The AAIP must include instructions and procedures for all installed equipment.

PART 121 AIR CARRIER INSPECTIONS

Air carriers operating under Part 121 must maintain their aircraft under a Continuous Airworthiness Maintenance Program (CAMP). A continuous airworthiness inspection program is one element of an overall CAMP. The basic requirements of a CAMP include inspection, scheduled and unscheduled maintenance, overhaul and repair, structural inspection, required inspection items (RII), and a reliability program. Specific instructions, standards, and operations specifications for each element of the continuous airworthiness maintenance program must be included in the air carrier's maintenance manual for the specific aircraft for which it is applicable. A CAMP is a fleet program and encompasses the entire group of aircraft versus inspection programs established for individual aircraft such as an AAIP, which is utilized under Part 135 air charter operations.

Like a progressive inspection program, the FAA must approve a continuous inspection program. This inspection program is extremely comprehensive, specific to the operator's aircraft, and requires complex maintenance facilities and large numbers of technical personnel. A continuous airworthiness inspection program is a program of FAA-approved inspection schedules which allow aircraft to be continually maintained in a condition of airworthiness without being taken out of service for long periods of time. This program keeps aircraft downtime to a minimum due to segmented maintenance or inspection intervals, thereby keeping the aircraft in service in a more efficient and convenient manner.

The continuous inspection program for a large air carrier may, as an example, consist of "letter check" inspection schedules. An example of a typical letter check inspection is outlined in figure 2-8. Letter checks are normally scheduled prior to due times or cycles. Over-flying due times or cycles of any required inspection is a direct violation of FAA regulations and may include large monetary fines.

It is difficult to provide an overall description of a general air carrier inspection program since each air carrier develops their own program and submits it to the FAA for approval. Hence, every air carrier operating in the U.S. utilizes a different CAMP designed specifically for its individual needs and specific flight operations. For detailed information regarding the CAMP, consult the specific air carrier's maintenance manual and operating specifications.

SPECIAL INSPECTIONS

Special inspections are scheduled inspections with prescribed intervals other than the normally established inspection intervals set out by the manufacturer. Special inspections may be scheduled by flight hours, calendar time, or aircraft cycles. For instance, in the case of a progressive inspection schedule for a small Cessna, special inspections occur at intervals other than 50, 100, or 200 hours. Special inspection items are usually explained in the notes section of the service manual inspection chapter.

Examples of special inspection items may include oil change information after an engine overhaul, the inspection and replacement of hoses at engine overhaul, and magnetic compass compensation every 1000 hours. Additionally, inspection and replacement of the rubber packings on each brake at 5-year intervals, and inspection and lubrication of the elevator trim tab actuator at 500-hour intervals may also constitute special inspection items specific to each model of aircraft.

ALTIMETER AND STATIC SYSTEMS AND CERTIFICATIONS

Altimeter and static system inspections are considered special inspections. Every aircraft operated in controlled airspace in instrument meteorological conditions (IMC) must have its altimeters and static systems inspected and certified for integrity and accuracy every 24 calendar months as required by 14 CFR Part 91.411.

MAINTENANCE CHECK SCHEDULE

CHECK	SCOPE	INTERVAL
Service check	Log book and maintenance forms review (for example: time control items). Exterior visual checks and routine aircraft servicing such as hydraulic fluids, engine oil, & general lubrication. Operational checks.	Required no more than 48 elapsed calendar hours from the last Service Check, A-1, A-2, A-3, A-4, or C check.
A Check: A-1 check A-2 check A-3 check A-4 check	Log book and maintenance forms review. Exterior visual check, routine and specific inspections, and routine aircraft servicing. Replacing time-limited items. Operational checks.	Required no more than 125 flight hours from the last equalized A and/or C check.
C Check	Includes "A: check items in addition to detailed inspections of aircraft, engines, components, and appliances.	Required no more than 3600 flight hours from the last C check.
D Check: D-1 check D-2 check D-3 check D-4 check	Includes "C" check items in addition to extensive dissasembly and opening up of the aircraft, and weight & balance. Flight test after operational checks.	Required to be performed at no more than 9000 flight hours or 3 calendar years, whichever occurs first from the last phase D check.

Figure 2-8. Typical air carrier maintenance "letter check" schedule outlining the scope and time intervals of required inspections for a specific type of aircraft. The maintenance schedule outline is used in conjunction with specific work cards that detail specific tasks to perform to maintain the airworthiness of the aircraft and all installed equipment.

The scope of the altimeter and static system certification is outlined in 14 CFR Part 43, Appendix E. The altimeter is checked for operation and accuracy up to the highest altitude it is used, usually the aircraft's service ceiling, and a record is made of this inspection and certification in the aircraft maintenance records.

The altimeter certification may be conducted by the manufacturer of the aircraft, or by a certificated repair station (CRS) holding an appropriate rating that authorizes this particular inspection. A certified airframe technician, however, may perform the static pressure system leakage tests and integrity determination but cannot perform the certification of the system.

ATC TRANSPONDER INSPECTIONS

Transponder inspections are also considered special inspections. The radar beacon transponder that is required for aircraft operating in most areas of controlled airspace must be inspected each 24 calendar months by any of the following: a certificated repair station approved for this type of inspection, a holder of a continuous-airworthiness maintenance program, or the manufacturer of the aircraft on which the transponder is installed. This test is required by 14 CFR Part 91.413 and its conduct is described in 14 CFR Part 43, Appendix F.

EMERGENCY LOCATOR TRANSMITTER

The Emergency Locator Transmitter (ELT) installed on most aircraft must also have a special inspection required every 12 months in accordance with 14 CFR Part 91.207. The inspection entails checking for proper installation, battery corrosion, operation of the controls and crash sensor, and the ELT signal. The battery's expiration date, which must be marked on the outside of the transmitter and recorded in the maintenance logs, must be checked for expiration.

OTHER SPECIAL INSPECTIONS

Other equipment that should be considered for special inspections might include life vests and life rafts (if installed), first aid supplies, and other similar items. These should be inspected at the specified intervals using the equipment manufacturer's instructions for continued airworthiness.

STUDY QUESTIONS

1. Who can approve a section of an approved inspection program to service after it has been completed?

2. If an annual inspection is performed on June 6, 1993, when will the inspection expire?

3. Can an annual inspection be signed off as completed in the maintenance records if the aircraft is unairworthy?

4. Who can perform an annual inspection?

5. What aircraft are required to have a 100 hour inspection?

6. Can an aircraft be legally flown if its annual inspection has expired? If so, how?

7. How many hours can a 100 hour inspection be exceeded if it is necessary to fly the aircraft to a place where the inspection can be performed?

8. Who can approve the aircraft for return to service after a 100-hour inspection?

9. What is the primary advantage of using the progressive inspection system for inspecting an aircraft?

Chapter 3
Inspection and Maintenance Documents

A large number of documents that must be consulted in order to maintain the airworthiness of an aircraft. Of these, some provide mandatory information that must be complied with to meet Federal regulations, while others are advisory in nature and serve to impart useful information to help inspection personnel perform their jobs more thoroughly. Some of the regulatory documentation includes Type Certificate Data Sheets, Airworthiness Directives, and manufacturer's FAA approved service information. Non-regulatory information includes Advisory Circulars, manufacturer's inspection and maintenance information, as well as others.

TYPE CERTIFICATE DATA SHEETS

As previously discussed, new airframes, powerplants, and appliances are issued a type certificate once they have been FAA approved. Type Certificate Data Sheets (TCDS) set forth essential factors and other conditions that are required for U.S. airworthiness certification. The TCDSs are provided in paper or microfiche form and are available from the Superintendent of Documents, U.S. Government Printing Office. In either format, TCDSs are available in 6 volumes as follows:

- Volume 1 — Single-Engine Airplanes
- Volume 2 — Small Multi-Engine Airplanes (Less than 12,500 pounds maximum certificated takeoff Weight).
- Volume 3 — Large Multi-Engine Airplanes
- Volume 4 — Rotorcraft, Gliders, Balloons, and Airships
- Volume 5 — Aircraft Engines and Propellers
- Volume 6 — Aircraft, Engine and Propeller Listings

Volume six of the TCDS contains information pertaining to older aircraft models, of which 50 or less are shown on the FAA Aircraft Registry. It also includes engine and propeller information for which approvals have expired or for which the manufacturer no longer holds a production certificate. Volume 6 is not subject to frequent revision, while the other five volumes are periodically revised to reflect new aircraft makes and models.

The type certificate number assigned to the product is also used on each Type Certificate Data Sheet, where both technical and general information concerning the product are found. The type certificate number, with the date and revision number of the data sheet, is enclosed in a box located in the upper right corner. [Figure 3-1]

An aircraft Type Certificate Data Sheet contains the information necessary for the proper maintenance and inspection of an aircraft or its associated equipment. Information contained in a TCDS is FAA approved data. Any deviation from the items listed in the data sheets is considered a major alteration and must be documented by a Major Repair or Alteration Form 337.

The Type Certificate Data Sheet is the primary source of information for:

- The type and model of approved engine(s) for the aircraft.
- The minimum fuel grade for the approved engine(s).
- The maximum approved rpm and the horsepower rating of the engine(s).
- Propellers approved for use, rpm limits, and operating restrictions, if any.
- Airspeed limits for the aircraft in knots and mph.
- Center of Gravity range, in inches from the datum.
- Empty weight center of gravity range may be listed, if it has been established by the manufacturer.
- Location of the reference datum line.
- All maximum weights allowed for various compartments and locations within the aircraft.
- Oil and fuel capacity and fuel tank moment arms.
- Control surface movements in degrees.
- Required equipment necessary for operation of the aircraft.
- Any additional equipment found that is necessary for certification of the aircraft.

Notes that are pertinent to all models of a particular aircraft design are contained toward the back of the Type Certificate Data Sheet. Within the notes section is information pertaining to:

3-1

DEPARTMENT OF TRANSPORTATION
FEDERAL AVIATION ADMINISTRATION

A12CE
Revision 11
BEECH
60
A60

May 7, 1973

TYPE CERTIFICATE DATA SHEET NO. A12CE

This data sheet which is part of type certificate No. A12CE prescribes conditions and limitations under which the product for which the type certificate was issued meets the airworthiness requirements of the Federal Aviation Regulations.

Type Certificate Holder   Beech Aircraft Corporation
Wichita, Kansas 67201

I - Model 60, 4 or 6 PCLM (Normal Category), Approved February 1, 1968
    Model A60, 4 or 6 PCLM (Normal Category), Approved January 30, 1970

Engines	Lycoming TI0-541-E1A4 or TI0-541-E1C4 (2 of either or 1 of each)
Fuel	100/130 minimum grade aviation gasoline
Engine limits	For all operations, 2900 r.p.m. (380 b. hp.)

Propeller and propeller limits	(a) Two (in any combination) Hartzell three-blade propellers
	    Diameter: 74 in., (Normal) Minimum allowable for repair 73 1/2 in.
	    (No further reduction permitted)
	    Pitch settings at 30 in. sta.:
	      low 14°, high 81.7°
	    HC-F 3 YR-2/C7479-2R
	or HC-F-3 YR-2/C7497B-2R
	or HC-F 3 YR-2F/FC 7479B-2R
	or HC-F 3 YR-2F/FC 7479B-2R
	(b) Beech 60-389000-3 governor

Airspeed limits		
	Never exceed	235 knots
	Maximum structural cruising	208 knots
	Maneuvering	161 knots
	Maximum flap extension speed	
	Approach position 15°	175 knots
	Full down position 30°	135 knots
	Landing gear extended	174 knots
	Landing gear operating	174 knots

C.G. range (landing gear extended)
    (+134.2) to (+139.2) at 6725 lb.
    (+128.0) to (+139.2) at 5150 lb. or less
    Straight line variation between points given
    Moment change due to retracting landing gear (+857 in.-lb.)

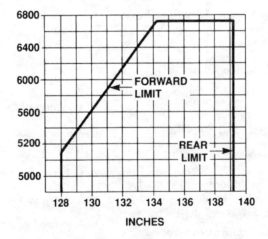

Empty wt. C.G. range	None	
Maximum weight	Takeoff and landing	6725 lb.
Ramp weight		6819 lb.

Figure 3-1. The Type Certificate Data Sheet for a particular aircraft model consists of many pages of information. Note that the TCDS contains information with regard to multiple models of the same basic aircraft design.

No. of seats	4 (2 at +141, 2 at +173) (add 2 at +205)				
Maximum baggage (structural limit)	500 lb. at +75 (nose compartment 655 lb. at +212 (aft area of cabin)				
Fuel capacity	142 gal. (+138) comprising two interconnected cells in each wing or 204 gal. (+139) comprising three cells in each wing and one cell in each nacelle (four cells interconnected) See NOTE 1 for data on system fuel				
Oil capacity (wet sump)	26 qt. (+88)				
Max. operating limit	30,000 ft. pressure altitude				
Control surface movements	Wing flaps			Maximum	30°
	Aileron	Up	25°	Down	15°
	Aileron tab (L.H. only)	Up	10°	Down	10°
	Aileron tab anti-servo	Up	12°	Down	7°
	Elevator	Up	17°	Down	15°
	Elevator tab (L.H. only)	Up	10°	Down	30°
	Elevator tab servo	Up	6°	Down	7°
	Rudder	Right	33°	Left	28°
	Rudder tab	Right	26°	Left	26°
Serial Nos. eligible	Model 60: P-3 thru P-126 (except P-123) Model A60: P-123, P-127 and up (see NOTE 3)				
Datum	Located 100 in. forward of front pressure bulkhead				
Leveling means	Drop plumb line between leveling screws in cabin door frame rear edge				
Certification basis	Part 23 of the Federal Aviation Regulations effective February 1, 1965 as amended by 1, 2, 3, and 12; and Special Conditions dated May 16, 1967, forwarded with FAA letter dated June 1, 1967; approved for flight into known icing conditions when equipped as specified in the approved airplane flight manual. Application for Type Certificate dated December 22, 1965. Type Certificate No. A12CE issued February 1, 1968, obtained by the manufacturer under delegation option procedures.				
Production basis	Production Certificate No. 8 issued and Delegation Option Manufacturer No. CE-2 authorized to issue airworthiness certificates under delegation option provisions of Part 21 of the Federal Aviation Regulations.				
Equipment	The basic required equipment as prescribed in applicable airworthiness regulations (see Certification basis) must be installed in the aircraft for certification. This equipment must include, for all operations, Airplane Flight Manual P/N 60-590000-5D dated January 15, 1971, amended July 1, 1971, or later issue.				

In addition:

1. For flights into known icing conditions, these flight manual supplements and the equipment noted therein:

   60-590001-17 Flight Into Known Icing Conditions.

   60-590001-11 Continuous Pressure Operated Surface Deice System.

   60-590001-13 Goodrich Electrothermal Propeller Deice System.

2. For all other operations:

   Pre-stall warning indicator P/N 151-6, 151-7, or 190-2 (Safe Flight Corporation).

Figure 3-1. Continued Part 2 of 3

> NOTE 1. Current weight and balance data including list of equipment included in certificated empty weight and loading instructions when necessary must be provided for each aircraft at the time of original certification.
>
> The certificated empty weight and corresponding center of gravity locations must include unusable fuel of 24 lb. at (+135).
>
> NOTE 2. The following placard must be displayed in front of and in clear view of the pilot:
>
> "This airplane must be operated in the normal category in compliance with the operation limitations stated in the form of placards, markings and manuals."
>
> NOTE 3. Fuselage pressure vessel structural life limit — refer to the latest revision of the Airplane Flight Manual for mandatory retirement time.
>
> NOTE 4. Model 60 (S/N P-3 thru P-126 except P-123) when modified to Beech dwg. 60-5008 and Model A60 (S/N P-123, P-127 and up) eligible for a masximum weight of 6775 lb.
>
> NOTE 5. A landing weight of 6435 lb. must be observed if 10 PR tires are installed on aircraft not equipped with 60-810012-15 (LH) or 60-810012-16 (RH) shock struts.
>
> . . . END . . .

Figure 3-1. Continued Part 3 of 3

- Any placards which must be displayed in full view of the pilot.
- If an FAA approved flight manual is required.
- Means to level the aircraft for weight and balance center-of-gravity determination.

The Type Certificate Data Sheet is used during required airworthiness inspections to ensure that an aircraft conforms to its type certificate. For example, a TCDS lists an aircraft's various airspeed limits. These limits must be marked on the face of the airspeed indicator in accordance with 14 CFR Part 23.1545. The technician performing the inspection must check these instrument markings to be sure they agree with those in the TCDS.

The TCDS also contains information required to perform a weight and balance check on an aircraft. For example, the leveling means, location of the datum, and the center of gravity range are listed in the data sheets and must be used in weight and balance computations. While a weight and balance check is seldom required during airworthiness inspections, the aircraft must be weighed and a weight and balance report reconstructed if the original documentation has become lost or destroyed.

AIRCRAFT SPECIFICATIONS

Prior to 1958, aircraft were certificated under the Civil Air Regulations (CARs). These regulations stipulated that information on certificated aircraft, engines, and powerplants be listed in aircraft specifications. The specifications were similar to Type Certificate Data Sheets with the addition of an equipment list. Many of the older specifications for one type aircraft often required up to sixty or seventy pages of information in the equipment list. The necessity of updating and revising the specifications became more costly and time consuming each year. Because of this, the equipment list was removed from the specifications and Type Certificate Data Sheets were issued for new aircraft and equipment under the provisions of 14 CFR Part 23. Newer aircraft are provided with an equipment list which is provided to the aircraft owner at time of delivery. This information is required to be carried on board the aircraft whenever it is operated in flight. Many of the newer aircraft models have the equipment list information included in a section of the FAA-approved Aircraft Flight Manual.

Aircraft that were originally certified with aircraft specifications do have the option of changing to the TCDS. Therefore, when conducting a conformity inspection or weight and balance check on an older aircraft that was originally certificated under the CARs, it may be necessary to look in both the aircraft specifications and the Type Certificate Data Sheets.

SUPPLEMENTAL TYPE CERTIFICATES

By meeting specific requirements, the FAA allows a product to deviate from its original type design. When an aircraft owner desires to alter an aircraft, one of the easiest methods for obtaining FAA approval is to apply for, and comply with, a Supplemental Type Certificate (STC). An STC prescribes the methods and techniques that, when properly performed, allows the aircraft to be approved for return to service without additional engineering and flight testing requirements. Other methods used to alter an aircraft are discussed in Chapter 6 — Major Repairs and Alterations.

An STC is issued in accordance with 14 CFR Part 21, Subpart E. Examples of STC approvals include converting an aircraft to use automotive gasoline, changes to another engine make and/or model, change of propeller models, or installing other equipment not originally certified on the aircraft.

When an originating STC has been applied for and obtained, the person or organization that holds the STC may offer the certificate and type design information to others desiring to perform the same alteration. In most cases, the holder of the STC charges a fee for the certificate and design change information. If an STC does not already exist for the desired change, or if a person or organization wishes to obtain their own STC, an application must be made to the FAA to evaluate the change and issue the appropriate certification. The STC approval process, however, requires the design change to meet the same requirements that an aircraft manufacturer must meet. This requires the change to be evaluated by the FAA in areas such as manufacturing, quality control, flight and ground tests, among many others.

The availability of existing STCs is published in the **Summary of Supplemental Type Certificates** and can be searched on the internet at WWW.FAA.GOV. Within the summary, a person can view a basic description of the alteration, and obtain the name and address of the STC holder. The person desiring to obtain the STC must contact the certificate holder to determine the terms and conditions for obtaining the certificate. By closely following the STC information, and documenting the STC number and methods of compliance on an FAA Form 337 — Major Alteration and Repair, the altered aircraft can be approved for return to service by an FAA inspector, an A&P technician holding an Inspection Authorization (IA), a certified repair station authorized to do the type of work, or others, as stipulated on the Form 337. [Figure 3-2 on page 3-6]

One problem that occurs with the incorporation of an STC is that the person performing the alteration must verify that its use does not conflict with other design changes. For example, if an aircraft has been modified by an STC approval process to install a higher horsepower engine, it may negate being able to use subsequent STC design changes where the desired change may impact the operation of the aircraft with the engine change. In these situations, it may be necessary for the aircraft to be evaluated for the effect of the subsequent change before being approved for return to service.

Another factor that must be considered with any design change by the use of an STC involves instructions for continued airworthiness. Again as an example, if an aircraft has had an engine change, instructions must be kept with the aircraft's permanent maintenance records, detailing the conditions that must be met to maintain the airworthiness of the aircraft. The conditions may include recommended overhaul times, the replacement requirements and limitations of life limited parts, etc. In most cases, an STC change also requires the Aircraft Flight Manual (AFM) to incorporate a supplement, addressing the conditions that must be adhered to regarding the operation of the aircraft.

Since each STC has its own unique criteria that must be met, a copy of the STC instructions should be retained with the aircraft's permanent maintenance records for future reference. Often, maintenance technicians must consult these instructions to determine what actions they need to take when maintaining the aircraft.

AIRWORTHINESS DIRECTIVES

An Airworthiness Directive (AD) is issued as an amendment to 14 CFR Part 39 and therefore must be complied with as stipulated within the text of the AD. Registered aircraft owners receive ADs from the FAA anytime a defect has been identified as being applicable to their make and model aircraft. The AD is sent directly to the owner at the address indicated on the aircraft registration certificate, or as updated in the FAA's database. When an AD is received, it is the owner or operator's responsibility to determine what actions must be taken to comply with the AD. It is also the responsibility of any person performing an airworthiness inspection to determine that all applicable ADs have been complied with before authorizing the aircraft to be returned to service.

ADs are issued and grouped as follows:

Airframes

Powerplants

Propellers

Appliances

United States of America
Department of Transportation—Federal Aviation Administration
Supplemental Type Certificate

Number AB123CD

This certificate, issued to John Doe Aircraft Services
1234 Airport Road
Anywhere, USA 12345-1000

certifies that the change in the type design for the following product with the limitations and conditions therefor as specified hereon meets the airworthiness requirements of Part 3 *of the* Civil Air Regulations.

Original Product—Type Certificate Number: 1A2
Make: Piper
Model: PA-18-135, PA-18A-135, PA-18S-135, PA-18AS-135, PA-18-150, PA-18A-150, PA-18S-150, PA-18AS-150.

Description of Type Design Change.

Installation of McCauley 1A175/GM 8241 propeller on the -135 models listed above, and installation of McCauley 1A175/GM8241 through GM8244 on the -150 models listed above per page 2 of Joe's Aircraft Services Instruction Sheet dated 20 October 1968 and amended 15 May 1969 and 7 January 1970.

Limitations and Conditions:

The approval of this change in type design applies basically to Piper PA-18 models only. This approval should not be extended to other aircraft of this model on which other previously approved modifications are incorporated unless it is determined by the installer that the interrelationship between this change and any of those other previously approved modifications will introduce no adverse effect on the airworthiness of that aircraft. This determination should include consideration of significant changes in weight distribution such as an increase in the fixed disposable weight in the fuselage.

This certificate and the supporting data which is the basis for approval shall remain in effect until surrendered, suspended, revoked, or a termination date is otherwise established by the Administrator of the Federal Aviation Administration.

Date of application: 1 September 1967
Date of issuance: 27 May 1968

Date amended: 9-20-68, 10-15-68, 5-12-69, 6-18-69, 1-8-70, and 8-4-71

By direction of the Administrator

Robert J. Smith
ROBERT J. SMITH, Chief
Engineering and Manufacturing Branch
Northern Region
(Title)

Any alteration of this certificate is punishable by a fine of not exceeding $1,000, *or imprisonment not exceeding 3 years, or both.*

This certificate may be transferred in accordance with FAR 21.47.

FAA Form 8110-2 (10-68)

Figure 3-2. Supplemental type certificates are available for aircraft owners who want to install an engine, propeller, or appliance that is not part of the original type certificate design. The STC comes from the certificate holder as a package, including all information necessary to make the modification, and in many cases, even includes component parts.

ADs are also available by subscription from the Superintendent of Documents, Government printing office, or can be accessed on-line at the FAA's web site. In subscription form, ADs are issued in two volumes, and revised on a bi-weekly cycle. Volume 1 contains information for small general aviation aircraft and appliances, while volume 2 pertains to larger aircraft and their appliances. [Figure 3-3]

ADs are also available on-line from the FAA's web site at WWW.FAA.GOV. Click on Regulatory/Advisory, Airworthiness Directives. By clicking on ADs by make, you will find an alphabetical list of all manufacturers of airframes, engines, propellers, and appliances that have ADs issued pertaining to their products. To start developing an AD compliance report, click on the first letter of the airframe manufacturer, and then select the specific manufacturer of the airframe. Next, select the model aircraft that you are researching. For example, a chronological list of ADs that apply to Cessna 172N airplanes is obtained by clicking on "172N". A list of all ADs that are applicable to the specific model aircraft is then retrieved, with links that take you directly to the text of the AD. [Figure 3-4 on page 3-8]

In addition to checking the specific airframe make and model, the AD check must include the ADs that pertain to all models of a specific type. For example, when checking the 172N ADs, you need to also check the ADs that pertain to the 172 series aircraft. These ADs are grouped at the beginning of the 172 model list.

Not all ADs in the list will require action, other than for an individual to make the determination as to why the AD does not require action. For example, the applicability statement of an AD may indicate that certain serial numbered aircraft are exempted. If the aircraft serial number is exempt, the AD is still considered to be applicable to the aircraft, but it does not require further action. As such, the AD should be itemized in a chronological list of applicable ADs, with a notation as to why the AD does not require action.

Once the airframe manufacturer's ADs have been researched, it is necessary to repeat the process for the engine, propeller, and all installed appliances (accessories). Typically, a separate chronological list is generated for each component, and entered into the appropriate maintenance record. The advantage to this is that if a component, such as the engine, is removed and sold, the transfer of records is easier with regard to the status of Airworthiness Directive compliance.

When researching the airframe, engine, and propeller ADs, the process is reasonably straight-forward since the make, model, and serial number of each component is readily obtained. Appliances, on the other hand, require a great degree of care and meticulous research to determine which ADs are applicable to a particular aircraft. For example, there are often ADs issued against fuel tanks, but the fuel tank information for the aircraft is not readily apparent. To help identify these types of components, it's advisable to have the aircraft's equipment list available during the research, or to have a separate record of the makes, models, and serial numbers of all appliances. Maintenance release tags for installed components may also provide information that is beneficial to the research. In extreme

82-06-11 R1 PIPER AIRCRAFT CORPORATION: Amendment 39-4349 as amended by Amendment 39-4408. Applies to the following airplanes certificated in any category.
Nose Landing Gear Inspection and Rigging
(Part I of Service Bulletin)

MODELS AFFECTED:	SERIAL NUMBERS AFFECTED:
PA-28R-201T Turbo Arrow III	28R-7703001 through 28R-7803373
PA-28RT-201T Turbo Arrow IV	28R-7931001 through 28R-8131193

Nose Landing Gear Inspection and Modification
(Part II of Service Bulletin)

MODELS AFFECTED:	SERIAL NUMBERS AFFECTED:
PA-28R-200 Arrow II	28R-7635522 through 28R-7635545
PA-28R-201 Arrow III	28R-7737001 through 28R-7837317
PA-28RT-201 Arrow IV	28R-7918001 through 28R-8118082

Figure 3-3. ADs are issued with a unique number. The first group of numbers indicates the year the AD was issued. The second group of numbers indicates the bi-weekly cycle during which the AD was issued, while the last numbers indicate the numerical order that the AD was issued within the bi-weekly cycle. For some ADs, the letter R followed by a number, indicates that the AD has been revised and reissued.

cases, however, it may be necessary to disassemble a portion of the aircraft to determine if an AD is applicable to the aircraft, and if so, what further action is required. [Figure 3-5]

81-07-11 R1 CESSNA: Amendment 39-4078 as amended by Amendment 39-4096. Applies to Model 335 (S/N 335-0001 thru 335-0065), Model 340 (S/N 340-0001 thru 340-0555) and Model 340A (S/N 340A0001 thru 340A1203) airplanes certificated in any category.

COMPLIANCE: Required as indicated, unless already accomplished.

To ensure the integrity of the elevator balance weight support structure and specified components of the horizontal stabilizer, accomplish the following:

A) Prior to further flight and at each 10 hours time-in-service interval thereafter, accomplish the following in accordance with Cessna Multi-engine Customer Care Service Information Letter ME79-44, Revision 5, dated September 29, 1980:

1. On all airplanes, remove the elevator tip covers and visually inspect the elevator balance weights for looseness.

a. On all Models 335 and 340 airplanes and on Model 340A (S/Ns 340A0001 thru 340A1038) airplanes, visually inspect the P/N 0832250-4, -33 and -75 ribs, and P/N 0832000-61, -62 gussets for cracks and/or loose rivets.

b. On Model 340A (S/Ns 340A1039 thru 340A1203) airplanes, visually inspect the P/N 832250-100 and -33 ribs, P/N 5334108-2 channel, -3 spar extension and -4 gussets for cracks and/or loose rivets.

2. Visually inspect the horizontal stabilizer outboard hinge bracket assembly (on Models 340 (all S/Ns) and 340A (S/Ns 340A0001 through 340A1035), the P/N is 5132013-5; on Model 340A (S/Ns 340A1036 thru 340A1203) the P/N is 5132013-10; and on Model 335 (all S/Ns) the P/N is 5132013-7), the outboard hinge bearing, the aft spar, and the tip ribs for cracks, loose rivets, or signs of chafing.

3. Prior to further flight, replace any defective parts found during any inspection required by this AD with airworthy parts of the same part number.

B) Within 24 hours following any inspection specified by paragraph A), the owner/operator must submit a written report of any cracks, loose rivets, or signs of chafing discovered during any inspection required by this AD to the Federal Aviation Administration, Aircraft Certification Program, Room 238, Terminal Building 2299, Mid-Continent Airport, Wichita, Kansas 67209. (Reporting approved by the Office of Management and Budget Order OMB No. 04-R0174.)

C) On or before December 15, 1981, replace the horizontal tail in accordance with Cessna Service Kit Instructions SK 340-24, dated March 16, 1981, and Cessna Service Kits SK 340-24-1, -2, or -3, and SK 340-19, as appropriate. After installation of the appropriate Cessna Service Kit(s), the requirements of paragraphs A) and B) of this AD are no longer applicable.

D) Airplanes may be flown in accordance with FAR 21.197 to a location where the provisions of paragraph C) of this AD can be accomplished.

E) Any equivalent method of compliance with this AD must be approved by the Chief, Aircraft Certification Program Office, Room 238, Terminal Building 2299, Mid-Continent Airport, Wichita, Kansas 67209; telephone (316) 942-4285.

This AD supersedes AD 80-21-04, Amendment 39-3959.

Amendment 39-4078 became effective April 13, 1981.

This amendment 39-4096 becomes effective April 17, 1981.

Figure 3-4. All newer ADs are produced in a consistent format as shown in this figure. Older ADs are issued in a similar format. Care must be taken to thoroughly read the body text of the AD to determine if action must be taken, and then how to comply with the AD when action is required.

AIRWORTHINESS DIRECTIVE RECORD

AIRCRAFT MAKE: MODEL: SERIAL NUMBER: N NUMBER:

AD NUMBER	DATE OF REVISION	SUBJECT	DATE OF COMPLIANCE	TOTAL TIME AT COMPLIANCE	METHOD OF COMPLIANCE	ONE TIME	RECURRING	NEXT DUE DATE/TIME	NAME SIGNATURE NUMBER
76-03-05	2-17-90	Bracket Installation	6-30-92	826 Hrs.	Install bracket i/a/w Para. b	x			*John M. Smith* John Smith A&P 00110000
76-05-04	7-12-90	Stab. Attach. Inspection	6-26-92	1248 Hrs.	Inspected Stab. Attach i/a/w Para. a & b		x	2248 Hrs.	*Robert B. Johnson* Robert Johnson A&P 110011000

Figure 3-5. The aircraft maintenance records must contain a chronological list indicating the status of all applicable ADs. Appliance AD lists are generally provided in the maintenance record for the component that they closest apply to. For example, an appliance AD regarding an ignition system magneto is best kept with the engine records.

ADVISORY CIRCULARS

Many of the technical publications and regulations issued by the FAA are complex in nature and often require additional explanation. As a result, the FAA issues Advisory Circulars (ACs) to inform, explain, and provide further guidance. Advisory circulars are informative only and cannot be used as approved data unless incorporated into a regulation or airworthiness directive. Advisory circulars are listed in numerical sequence which closely follows the same subject areas covered by the Parts of 14 CFR. Some of the subject areas are:

- 00 General
- 10 Procedural Rules
- 20 Aircraft
- 60 Airmen
- 120 Air Carriers, Air Travel Clubs, and Operators for Compensation and Hire; Certification and Operations.

Within the general subject areas are more specific subjects that are assigned a unique number. For example, within the general subject of Aircraft, the specific subject of maintenance, preventive maintenance, and rebuilding and alterations is assigned the number 43, which is also the number of the FAR Part that covers maintenance.

One of the most popular Advisory Circulars for maintenance technicians is in the AC 43 series. AC43.13-1B and -2A, *Acceptable Methods, Techniques and Practices*, is a highly technical publication covering most of the aircraft maintenance areas which an Aviation Maintenance Technician must service. It contains information on standard hardware and torque values, acceptable repair methods, and inspection techniques. [Figure 3-6]

To increase aviation safety, the FAA gathers information on mechanical problems and difficulties discovered by aviation maintenance technicians working in the field. When encountering a new or unusual maintenance problem, the technician is requested to fill out and mail an FAA Form 8010-4 Malfunction or Defect Report detailing the problem. When the FAA detects a trend forming with a particular aircraft or appliance, it publishes this information in AC43-16A *Aviation Maintenance Alerts*. Alerts are issued monthly to distribute the information gathered with the goal of improving service reliability. [Figure 3-7]

For a complete listing of ACs, the FAA publishes an advisory circular checklist. Periodically, the Advisory Circular Checklist (AC00-2) is revised and reissued to inform you of the current status of all ACs. The checklist also provides you with pricing and ordering information.

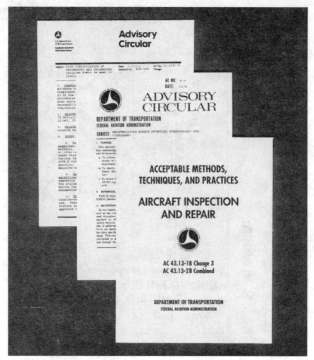

Figure 3-6. The FAA issues Advisory Circulars to explain or clarify the Federal Aviation Regulations. Advisory Circulars are non-regulatory in nature unless incorporated into a regulation and generally do not contain approved data.

Some ACs are free while others are available at cost. You can order either type through the U.S. Government Printing Office, as described in the checklist.

MANUFACTURER'S PUBLICATIONS

Aircraft manufacturers provide various manuals and service publications with their products to assist

Figure 3-7. Aviation Maintenance Alerts inform the general public, and especially personnel assigned to perform airworthiness inspections, of issues regarding aircraft safety that have been reported to the FAA.

technicians in inspection, maintenance, and repair. With few exceptions, the manufacturer's information is considered acceptable data for FAA purposes, but since the FAA does not review all of the material, it is not considered to be approved data unless specifically noted by the FAA. Where FAA approval has been granted, there will be a page or information block containing the signature of an authorized FAA representative.

The manufacturer's information is usually the best source of guidance material for maintaining an aircraft. In most situations, the FAA directs that the manufacturer's information to be used in the conduct of maintenance. Where necessary, however, the FAA may deem that the work must meet specific FAA guidelines, and therefore the use of the procedures presented in the publication must be formally approved. For example, if an Airworthiness Directive is issued against a product, the FAA may direct the manufacturer's maintenance instructions to be adhered to as part of the AD compliance. In this type of situation, the FAA has specifically reviewed the manufacturer's information and approved its use.

When working on any aircraft, personnel should become familiar with the general content of each type of publication that the manufacturer produces. In addition, manufacturers periodically revise these publications, and so it is important to verify that the manuals and service instructions are kept current. In most cases, the only way to determine the revision status of a publication is to consult the aircraft manufacturer. To disseminate the revision status of their publications, most manufacturers publish separate memoranda to provide this information.

ATA SPECIFICATION 100

At one time, the organization of data in manufacturer's publications was left up to the individual producing the manual. As a result, there was little uniformity among different publications, and much time was wasted as technicians had to learn each manufacturer's particular system. To correct this, the Air Transport Association of America (ATA) issued specifications for the organization of manufacturer's technical data. The ATA specification calls for the organization of an aircraft's technical data into individual systems which are numbered. Each system also has provisions for subsystem numbering. For example, all of the technical information on the fire protection system has been designated to be compiled under Chapter 26 under the ATA 100 specifications, with fire detection equipment further identified by the sub-chapter number 2610, and fire extinguishing equipment as 2620. Because of this specification, maintenance information for all transport, and many general aviation aircraft is arranged in the same way. [Figure 3-8]

Although manufacturer's maintenance manuals are written primarily for A and P mechanics use, they contain a wealth of information that other personnel also find beneficial. Some of the ATA Chapter codes that all aviation personnel should become familiar with for their appropriate aircraft include:

- Chapter 5 — Time Limits/Maintenance Checks (including life limited parts and manufacturer's airworthiness inspection programs)
- Chapter 6 — Dimensions and Areas
- Chapter 9 — Towing and Taxiing
- Chapter 10 — Parking & Mooring
- Chapter 11 — Placards & Markings
- Chapter 12 — Servicing

Most all newly manufactured aircraft follow the ATA Specification 100 format, while many manufacturers have, or are, in the process of converting the maintenance documentation for their older equipment to the ATA format.

MAINTENANCE/SERVICE MANUALS

Manufacturers produce the documentation necessary to maintain the serviceability of their products, but the titles and content of the publications vary between manufacturers. For example, some maintenance manuals detail servicing, inspection, and repair information within one text, while other manufacturers provide two separate manuals; one for servicing, and another for repair type work. A Structural Repair Manual (SRM) is another publication that may be used, which primarily provides dimensions, equipment, and techniques for performing major structural repair work. Some manufacturers incorporate this type of information under a separate chapter within their maintenance manuals, while others provide the separate SRM publication.

Maintenance manuals are also produced for each major assembly within an aircraft. For example, for a given reciprocating-engine airplane, there are usually maintenance manuals available for the airframe, powerplant, and propeller. In addition, maintenance manuals often exist for subassembly components such as the landing gear, starter motors, alternators, and other similar components.

A typical maintenance manual provides information on routine servicing, systems descriptions and functions, handling procedures, and component removal and installation. In addition, these manuals contain basic repair procedures and troubleshooting guides for common malfunctions. Maintenance information in these manuals is considered acceptable data by the FAA, except where specifically approved, as previously discussed. The manufacturer's maintenance

System	Sub	Title	System	Sub	Title	System	Sub	Title
21	00	AIR CONDITIONING		50	Steering	57	00	WINGS
	10	Compression		60	Position & Warning		10	Main Frame
	20	Distribution		70	Supplementary Gear		20	Auxiliary
	30	Pressurization Control	33	00	LIGHTS		30	Plates/Skin
	40	Heating		10	Flight Compartment		40	Attach Fittings
	50	Cooling		20	Passenger Compartment		50	Flight Surfaces
	60	Temperature Control		30	Cargo & Service Compartment	61	00	PROPELLERS-General
	70	Humidity Regulation		40	Exterior		10	Propeller Assembly
22	00	AUTO PILOT		50	Emergency Lighting		20	Controlling
	10	Amplification	34	00	NAVIGATION		30	Braking
	20	Actuation		10	Air Data Instrumentation		40	Indicating
	30	Controlling		20	Altitude & Direction Inst.	65	00	ROTORS
	40	Indicating		30	Radio Navigation		10	Main rotor
	50	Sensing		40	Radar Navigation		20	Anti-Torque Rotor Assy.
	60	Coupling		50	Proximity Warning		30	Accessory Driving
23	00	COMMUNICATIONS		60	Position Computing		40	Controlling
	10	HF	35	00	OXYGEN		50	Braking
	20	VHF		10	Crew		60	Indicating
	30	PA & Pass. Entertainment		20	Passenger	71	00	POWER PLANT
	40	Interphone		30	Portable		10	Cowling
	50	Audio Integrating	36	00	PNEUMATIC		20	Mounts
	60	Static Discharging		10	Distribution		30	Fireseals
	70	Voice Recorders		20	Indicating		40	Attach Fitting
24	00	ELECTRICAL POWER	37	00	VACUUM		50	Electrical Harness
	10	Generator Drive		10	Distribution	72	00	ENGINE TURBINE
	20	AC Generation		20	Indicating		10	Reduction Gear & Shaft Sect.
	30	DC Generation	38	00	WATER/WASTE		20	Air Inlet Section
	40	External Power		10	Potable		30	Compressor Section
	50	Elect. Load Distribution		20	Wash		40	Combustion Section
25	00	EQUIP./FURNISHINGS		30	Waste Disposal		50	Turbine Section
	10	Flight Compartment		40	Air Supply		60	Accessory Drives
	20	Passenger Compartment	49	00	AIRBORNE AUX. POWER		70	By-Pass Section
	30	Buffet/Galley		10	Power Plant	73	00	ENGINE FUEL & CONTROL
	40	Lavatory		20	Engine		10	Distribution
	50	Cargo & Accessory Compartment		30	Engine Fuel & Control		20	Controlling
	60	Emergency		40	Ignition Starting		30	Indicating
26	00	FIRE PROTECTION		50	Air	74	00	IGNITION
	10	Detection		60	Engine Controls		10	Electrical Power Supply
	20	Extinguishing		70	Indicating		20	Distribution
27	00	FLIGHT CONTROLS		80	Exhaust		30	Switching
	10	Aileron & Tab		90	Oil	75	00	AIR
	20	Rudder & Tab	51	00	STRUCTURES		10	Engine Anti-Icing
	30	Elevator & Tab	52	00	DOORS		20	Accessory Cooling
	40	Horiz. Stabilizer Control		10	Passenger/Crew		30	Compressor Control
	50	Flaps		20	Emergency Exit		40	Indication
	60	Spoiler & Drag		30	Cargo	76	00	ENGINE CONTROLS
	70	Gust Lock & Dampener		40	Service		10	Power Control
	80	Lift Augmenting		50	Fixed Interior		20	Emergency Shutdown
28	00	FUEL		60	Entrance Stairs	77	00	ENGINE INDICATING
	10	Storage		70	Door Warning		10	Power
	20	Distribution		80	Landing Gear		20	Temperature
	30	Dump	53	00	FUSELAGE		30	Analyzers
	40	Indications		10	Main Frame	78	00	EXHAUST
29	00	HYDRAULIC POWER		20	Auxiliary Structure		10	Collector
	10	Main		30	Plates, Skins		20	Noise Suppressor
	20	Auxiliary		40	Attach Fittings		30	Thrust Reverser
	30	Indicating		50	Cones & Fillets/Fairings	79	00	OIL
30	00	ICE & RAIN PROTECTION	54	00	NACELLES/PYLONS		10	Storage
	10	Airfoil		10	Main Frame		20	Distribution
	20	Air Intakes		20	Auxiliary Structure		30	Indicating
	30	Pitot and Static		30	Plates/Skin	80	00	STARTING
	40	Windows & Windshields		40	Attach Fittings		10	Cranking
	50	Antennas & Radomes		50	Fillets/Fairings		20	Igniting
	60	Propellers/Rotors	55	00	STABILIZERS	81	00	TURBINES
	70	Water Lines		10	Horizontal		10	Power Recovery
	80	Detection		20	Elevator		20	Turbo-Supercharger
31	00	INSTRUMENTS		30	Vertical	82	00	WATER INJECTION
	10	Panels		40	Rudder		10	Storage
	20	Independent Instruments		50	Attach Fittings		20	Distribution
32	00	LANDING GEAR	56	00	WINDOWS		30	Dumping & Purging
	10	Main & Doors		10	Flight Compartment		40	Indicating
	20	Nose & Doors		20	Cabin	83	00	ACCESSORY GEAR BOXES
	30	Extension & Retraction		30	Door		10	Drive Shaft Section
	40	Wheels and Brakes		40	Inspection & Observation		20	Gearbox Section

Figure 3-8. To ensure uniformity in maintenance documentation, ATA codes are assigned to all aircraft systems and subsystems. For example, all brake systems fall under the ATA 32-40 code.

manual material, however, may be used as substantiating data for gaining FAA approval for repairs and alterations.

OVERHAUL MANUAL

Manufacturers of airframes and components, such as engines, landing gear, hydraulic actuators, and other subassembly products often produce overhaul manuals to provide complex overhaul instructions. By definition, an overhaul consists of the following actions:

- Disassembly
- Cleaning
- Inspection
- Repair (as required)
- Reassembly
- Testing after reassembly

Each of these actions is covered in an overhaul manual and must be performed before an item can be considered overhauled. Use of this manual is required during any overhaul, and any maintenance release approving the component for return to service should include the part and revision number of the publication.

ILLUSTRATED PARTS CATALOG

An illustrated parts catalog (IPC) shows the location and part numbers of items installed on an aircraft, or used in a subassembly component. IPCs exist for all components including the airframe, powerplant, propeller, and their subassemblies.

The IPC contains multiple assembly drawings and part number references. They contain detailed exploded views of all areas of an aircraft to assist technicians in locating parts. Care should be taken to become familiar with any coding systems that the manufacturer uses to identify quantities of parts, and applicability of part numbers for specific models and serial numbered aircraft. [Figure 3-9]

WIRING DIAGRAM MANUALS

The majority of aircraft electrical systems and their components are illustrated in individual wiring manuals.

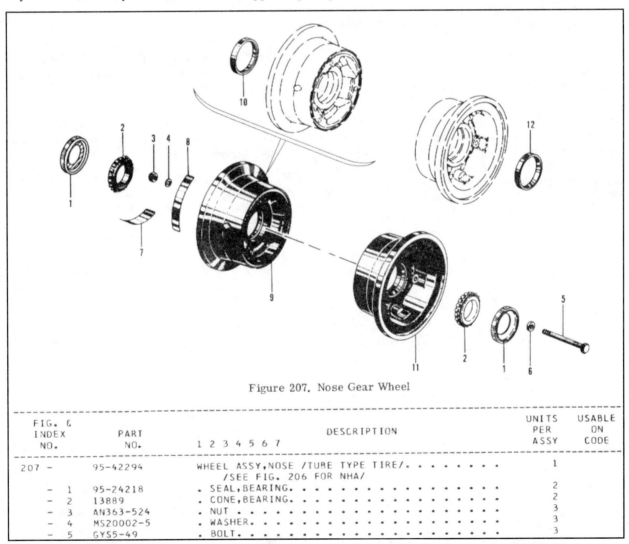

Figure 3-9. A typical page of an Illustrated Parts Catalog provides a detailed drawing of an aircraft part, and a list of part numbers identifying the subassemblies. Special notes and codes are provided within a table to indicate applicability to specific aircraft.

These manuals primarily provide schematic diagrams to aid in electrical system maintenance and troubleshooting. They also list part numbers and locations of electrical system components.

SERVICE INFORMATION

One way manufacturers communicate with aircraft owners, operators, and technicians is through service information publications or communiqué. This information, while generally not mandatory, is extremely important to comply with to retain equipment reliability.

Service information may also include suggestions for increased efficiency in maintaining an aircraft by providing more detailed procedural instructions with regard to a topic that has proven difficult as presented in the maintenance manual. This information, for example, includes service instructions that provide expanded troubleshooting and adjustment procedures for a fuel injection system for a particular model aircraft.

Other types of service information include the announcement of the availability of kits that allow for the modification of an aircraft. These kit modifications are often FAA approved and come complete with all parts and detailed instructions.

Of all service publications, the most vital involves the dissemination of flight safety information. Cessna Aircraft Company, for example, issues Service Bulletins, which convey information regarding a wide variety of critical topics. An example may include instructions for detecting and identifying defective components that may have been installed in the aircraft during the manufacturing process.

Often, because of the critical nature of these publications, the manufacturer may stipulate that compliance with the bulletin is mandatory. It should be noted, however, that the manufacturer does not have the authority to enforce action. On the other hand, if the FAA regards that the bulletin is critical, they may issue an Airworthiness Directive to make its compliance regulatory. Also, if an aircraft is covered by a warranty, non-compliance with a manufacturer's mandatory service publication may void the warranty.

STUDY QUESTIONS

1. Which volume of the Type Certificate Data Sheets would you look to find the approved engines for a small multi-engine airplane?

2. What do the numbers -05 represent in the AD number 99-02-05?

3. List the information that should be included in a maintenance release detailing compliance with an AD.

4. What documentation can be used to determine what appliances and components are installed on a specific aircraft when performing an AD conformity check for appliances?

5. Under what conditions are all aircraft required to be in compliance with a manufacturer's mandatory service action?

Chapter 4

Inspection Standards and Procedures

INSPECTION PERFORMANCE STANDARDS

The inspection of an aircraft to determine its airworthiness requires a great amount of skill and judgment. For the most part, the items to be inspected are usually listed in a checklist provided by the manufacturer of the aircraft. But how well an item is inspected or in what order, is up to the inspector. The determination of the airworthiness of an item is sometimes easy to ascertain using guidance material provided by the manufacturer, while at other times it is left up to the judgment of the individual. Component parts of an aircraft must also be checked to determine that they meet FAA standards, as well as being legal for installation on the aircraft. These factors, combined together, make it necessary for the inspector to develop a structured system or procedure that can be used to effectively inspect an aircraft.

It is essential that inspectors develop a set of standards for themselves so they may effectively determine if an item is airworthy. These standards must be high enough to guarantee the airworthiness of the aircraft, but yet not so high as to cause needless expense for the aircraft owner. The inspector must also withstand the pressures that may be applied by others to lower those standards and represent items airworthy when they are not. Once these standards are compromised, it is very difficult for an inspector to restore his or her integrity.

Aircraft owners and operators should also understand the role and responsibilities of the inspector. While the inspector primarily determines that an aircraft is in a safe condition for continued operation, they also provide services that help maintain the value of the aircraft. As such, the inspector requires all unairworthy items to be corrected, but also recommends or performs other maintenance that, while not required, improves the aircraft's appearance or helps to avert future problems.

INSPECTION PERFORMANCE RULES

Each person performing a 100-hour, annual, or progressive inspection shall perform those inspections in such a manner as to determine whether the aircraft concerned meets all applicable airworthiness requirements. This statement is a part of 14 CFR Part 43.15 and means that the aircraft must be physically airworthy. It must conform to its type certificate and manufacturer's specifications, comply with all applicable airworthiness directives, and be in condition for safe flight. [Figure 4-1]

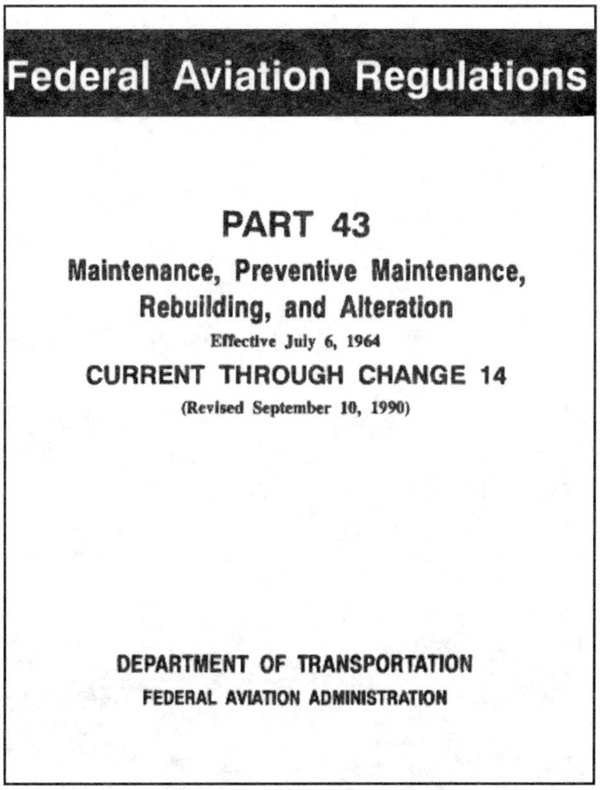

Federal Aviation Regulations

PART 43

Maintenance, Preventive Maintenance, Rebuilding, and Alteration

Effective July 6, 1964

CURRENT THROUGH CHANGE 14

(Revised September 10, 1990)

DEPARTMENT OF TRANSPORTATION
FEDERAL AVIATION ADMINISTRATION

Figure 4-1. 14 CFR Part 43 is the primary reference publication for the performance rules for conducting maintenance, including inspections.

All aircraft being maintained under an approved inspection program must also meet the requirements of 14 CFR Part 43.13. This regulation states that each person maintaining, altering, or performing preventive maintenance, shall use methods, techniques, and practices acceptable to the FAA. They shall use the tools, equipment, and test apparatus necessary to ensure completion of the work in accordance with accepted industry practices. If special equipment or test apparatus is recommended by the manufacturer involved, they must use that equipment or its equivalent acceptable to the FAA.

CHECKLIST REQUIREMENTS

Each person performing an annual or 100-hour inspection must use a checklist while performing an inspection. This checklist may be of the person's own design, one provided by the manufacturer of the equipment being inspected, or one obtained from another source. This checklist must include the scope and detail of the items listed in Appendix D of 14 CFR Part 43. If it is a rotorcraft, the items are listed in Paragraph b of 14 CFR Part 43.15.

FUNCTIONAL CHECKS REQUIRED

When a 100-hour or annual inspection is completed and before the aircraft can be approved for return to service, the engines must be run and checked for the following: [Figure 4-2]

1. Static (stationary aircraft) power check.
2. Idle RPM.
3. Magnetos and ignition system.
4. Fuel pressure, if equipped with a fuel pressure gage.
5. Oil pressure.
6. Oil temperature.
7. Cylinder temperature if equipped with a cylinder temperature gage.
8. All other operating systems for meeting the manufacturers' specifications.

Figure 4-2. After a 100-hour or an annual inspection, functional checks are required before approving an aircraft for return to service.

ROTORCRAFT PERFORMANCE RULES

When performing a 100-hour, annual, or progressive inspection on a rotorcraft, the following items are listed as specific inspection items in Paragraph b of 14 CFR Part 43.15.

1. The drive shafts or similar systems.
2. The main rotor transmission gear box for obvious defects.
3. The main rotor and center section (or the equivalent area).
4. The auxiliary rotor on helicopters.

These items are to be inspected in accordance with the manufacturer's maintenance manual and must comply with all other inspection requirements of the maintenance manual. [Figure 4-3]

Figure 4-3. When inspecting rotorcraft, specific inspection items are listed in 14 CFR Part 43.15.

INSPECTION PROCEDURES

The inspection of an aircraft requires that the person performing the inspection organizes their work so that the inspection can be performed in a logical and orderly sequence. This ensures that the aircraft is properly inspected with little chance that any item will be overlooked or forgotten. The accepted method of performing an inspection used by the aircraft maintenance industry also includes the service and repair activities necessary to return the aircraft to service. Including these activities into a procedure requires that the inspector follow an organized plan in completing the inspection.

The inspection of the aircraft is divided into basically five identifiable phases, as follows:

PRE-INSPECTION PHASE

The pre-inspection phase begins when the owner of the aircraft requests the services of a shop or an individual to perform an inspection on the aircraft. This phase includes the completion of a work order.

The work order serves as an agreement between the maintenance facility and the aircraft owner. If problems arise during or after the maintenance operation, the work order serves as a legal document to indicate the work that was authorized and performed. Throughout the inspection process, the work order should be amended to indicate any changes in the scope of the original agreement. For example, an initial work order agreement will usually indicate that the owner has agreed that an inspection is to be performed. Before any repairs are done, however, the additional costs and time factors should be discussed with the owner, and the work order amended and signed to indicate acceptance of the additional operations and costs.

While initially filling out the work order, the technician should interview the owner to determine if there are any obvious items that the owner wants corrected or checked. Since the technician is seldom able to analyze in-flight discrepancies first-hand, it is important that owners effectively communicate all indications associated with the discrepancy. If the aircraft is legal for flight, however, it may be advantageous for the owner to duplicate the discrepancy during flight with the technician aboard.

Once the work order has been filled out and the owner interview has been completed, maintenance record research should be done. This includes a check for past work performed, any performance trends as indicated through items such as engine compression checks, landing gear problems and service history, and other prominent indicators of historical problem areas.

Airworthiness Directive and service bulletin status should be checked next. This includes research into any recurring ADs, as well as determining if there are any new ADs that require action. Remember that AD research includes the airframe, powerplant, propeller (if applicable) and all installed appliances. Before the aircraft is disassembled for inspection, it is best to organize a work plan that includes AD actions that should be taken while the aircraft is open. If AD actions become apparent during this phase, the owner should also be advised and the work order amended accordingly.

A functional check should then be performed to confirm the powerplant operation. During the run-up, record engine indication values for maximum static- and idle-RPM, manifold pressure, oil pressure and temperature, cylinder head temperature, etc.

The technician should then perform a preliminary visual inspection to determine if there are any obvious discrepancies. This includes removing the cowling and looking for fuel and oil stains. These items should be noted on a discrepancy reporting form to be further checked during the inspection. [Figure 4-4]

From this point, inspection plates, interior seats, carpet, and upholstery should be removed as required to gain suitable access to perform a thorough visual inspection. Most manufacturers' maintenance manuals provide charts or tables to indicate which inspection panels to remove.

14 CFR Part 43 Appendix D also specifies that the aircraft must be thoroughly cleaned before conducting an inspection. Many shops and technicians will perform an initial cleaning before starting an inspection, but in most cases an aircraft requires further cleaning before each area is inspected.

At this point, tools and equipment are made ready, and any known parts that will be needed are ordered.

Figure 4-4. During the "pre-inspection phase", removal of aircraft cowling is necessary. Before cleaning, note any fluid or exhaust stains on the inside of the cowling and note their location for later inspection.

LOOK PHASE

The look phase is the actual inspection of the aircraft. It consists of looking, feeling, checking, measuring, operating, moving, testing, and whatever else is needed to determine the condition of the aircraft and its components. The checklist should be used with a planned sequence or order in which the various items of the aircraft are inspected.

Discrepancies and needed service that become apparent are recorded during this phase of the inspection. Interrupting the inspection to perform repairs and service should be avoided as much as possible at this point. The necessary repair and service items should be accomplished after the complete aircraft and engine has been inspected, or assigned to other individuals to perform, allowing the inspector or inspection team to remain focused on completing the inspection phase.

The primary purpose of the look phase is to determine the physical airworthiness of the aircraft and its components. All of the other activities included in the inspection of the aircraft are dependent upon, and in support of, the look phase of the inspection. [Figure 4-5]

Figure 4-5. During the "look phase" of an inspection, the technician looks, feels, checks, measures, operates, and moves whatever is needed to determine the physical condition of the aircraft and its components.

SERVICE AND REPAIR PHASE

The service and repair phase of the inspection is the necessary maintenance that is required to return the aircraft to service and keep it in airworthy condition until the next inspection. This service consists of many items such as lubricating wheel bearings, moving parts and control surface hinge bearings, as well as replacing and cleaning filters and screens, adding fluids in the brake and hydraulic reservoirs, and servicing the battery. The repair phase includes replacement, repair, and overhaul of the aircraft components and systems that are determined to be in an unairworthy condition.

FUNCTIONAL CHECK PHASE

Before an aircraft can be approved for return to service after any maintenance, a technician should conduct functional or operational checks on the aircraft or systems that have been serviced or repaired. Before a 100-hour or annual inspection can be approved for return to service, the person that approves the aircraft for return to service must run the aircraft engine(s) to determine that they will perform in accordance with the manufacturer's recommendations of power output (static and idle RPM), magnetos, fuel and oil pressure, and cylinder and oil temperatures. This is a requirement that is directed by 14 CFR Part 43.15 which is a minimum functional check required on most engine installations. Additional checks are usually recommended to ensure that all of the systems installed in a particular aircraft or engine are in airworthy condition according to the manufacturers' specifications. [Figure 4-6]

Figure 4-6. In the "functional test phase" a technician often runs the aircraft engines to determine if they meet the manufacturer's recommended performance specifications.

RETURN TO SERVICE PHASE

After an inspection and/or maintenance and before an aircraft can be legally flown, certain statements or notations must be made in the maintenance records and signed by an appropriately rated mechanic. The approved for return to service statement, along with the inspector's signature and certificate number serves the approval process.

A typical return to service entry for a 100-hour inspection consists of the date, aircraft total time in service, a brief description of the maintenance and service performed on the aircraft, and a record of compliance with any Airworthiness Directives or service bulletins performed during the inspection. This would be followed by the statement "I certify that this aircraft has been inspected in accordance with a 100-hour inspection and was determined to be in airworthy condition". This would be followed by the signature and certificate number of the person that performed the inspection, indicating that the aircraft meets regulatory requirements and is approved for return to service. It should be noted, however, that part of the inspection requirements also includes researching and updating a cumulative status list of ADs. This record must be thoroughly researched and signed by the inspector. While the cumulative list is generally kept separate from the inspection sign-off, it is still a vital component of the airworthiness inspection, and must be retained with the aircraft's maintenance records for at least one year, or until the work is superseded by another inspection.

PARTS APPROVALS

Throughout the inspection process, the inspector must diligently look for unapproved parts. In addition, the inspector must identify and replace parts and components that while being FAA approved, are incorrect for that particular aircraft. The wrong part may have been installed by a certificated mechanic that made an improper substitution or possibly by a person that was not properly certificated to perform the installation.

The parts used, from the smallest nuts and bolts, to major subassemblies such as landing gear, electric motors, lights, and all other components must meet specific standards established by the FAA. Replacement parts are often procured through vendors that perform the "middle man" functions of distribution to the end user. Their parts come from a variety of sources including the original equipment manufacturer (OEM), a company authorized to make replacement parts through an FAA Parts Manufacturer Approval (PMA), the manufacturer of a part that meets FAA Technical Standard Orders (TSO), surplus parts supply companies, and many others. When a technician obtains replacement parts, it is up to that individual, or a person within an organization assigned to the task, to determine that all parts received are procured from a reputable vendor. These vendors often provide support documentation that discloses the source of where the part was manufactured or distributed. At present there is no requirement for a set method of tracking this information, but there are a number of industry accepted practices that vendors take to help control the migration of unapproved or bogus parts into the supply network.

All persons involved in aircraft maintenance should be aware of the serious consequences that may occur when illegal parts enter aviation commerce. Obviously, the main reason bogus parts must be identified and isolated is to retain safety. Ultimately though, it should be realized that the business of manufacturing and disseminating bogus parts is propelled by greed, and is only controlled by the integrity of people that strive to maintain high ethical standards.

HARDWARE STANDARDS

All hardware used in aircraft construction must meet certain quality standards established by the manufacturer, which ultimately must meet FAA requirements. Screws, nuts, bolts, and rivets are only a small portion of the types of hardware used. Each item must be manufactured using the proper materials, machined to the correct tolerances and dimensions, and checked for quality before being approved for aircraft use. To maintain quality, the FAA requires all hardware to be manufactured to established standards. Some of the more common standards include Air Force-Navy Standards (AN), Military Standards (MS), Military Specifications (Mil-Spec), and National Aerospace Standards (NAS), among many others.

In most cases, a technician or repair facility procures a part from a vendor of their choosing. At other times, the aircraft owner may locate and obtain parts for use on their aircraft. Aircraft owners however, should understand that the technician or repair facility can be held liable if bogus parts are installed on an aircraft. When a part is provided through a source other than from the organization doing the work, tracking documentation should be retained to support that the part is FAA-approved. This may be shown by a maintenance release document, such as a serviceable tag, or another form that indicates the condition of the part as being airworthy and approved for in service use.

PARTS MANUFACTURER APPROVAL

A PMA authorizes a manufacturer, other than the original manufacturer, to produce replacement parts. These parts include items such as brake pads and disks, spark plugs, oil filters, and a wide assortment of others. In obtaining a PMA, the manufacturer of the part must show that the item meets the same standards specified for the original part. In addition, the part manufacturer must have in place, a method of assuring quality and tracking the manufacturing process. Tracking is required in the event a discrepancy is discovered wherein parts must be identified in order to inform end users of corrective actions that must be taken.

When a part is PMA approved, the manufacturer must indicate that it has met FAA PMA approval. This is usually done on a tag or label that is affixed to the product. If the tag becomes illegible or missing, the part cannot be assumed to be approved.

TECHNICAL STANDARD ORDERS

The FAA also prescribes a set of standards that various aircraft appliance and component manufacturers must meet to satisfy regulations specifying minimum performance and quality requirements. These standards are presented in Technical Standard Orders (TSO). A TSO is a minimum performance standard for specifying materials, parts, and appliances used on civil aircraft. When authorized to manufacture a material, part, or appliance to a TSO standard, this is referred to as TSO authorization. Receiving a TSO authorization is both design and production approval.

One example of a TSO authorized appliance applies to newer emergency locator transmitters that broadcast on 406 MHz. In order for a new ELT to be installed in an aircraft after June 21, 1995 the ELT must meet the requirements of TSO C-126. Before that date, an ELT had to meet the requirements of TSO C-91a. The older ELTs are authorized to remain in aircraft if they were originally installed in the aircraft before that date.

TSO C-126 provides many specifications including the manufacturing minima, performance requirements, activation system reliability, as well as many others.

A small sample of other common TSOs includes the following:

- TSO-C3d Turn and Slip Instruments
- TSO-C5e Direction Instrument, Non-Magnetic (Gyroscopically Stabilized)
- TSO-C9c Automatic Pilots
- TSO-C22g Safety Belts
- TSO-C74c Airborne Transponder Equipment
- TSO-C145 Global Positioning Systems

Other TSO authorizations can be obtained on the internet from the FAA's web site at WWW.FAA.GOV.

SURPLUS/SALVAGE PARTS

Surplus and salvaged parts are sometimes obtained for use on civil aircraft. While this is not necessarily illegal, it presents some problems that aviation personnel must be aware of. For example, many times these parts are obtained without support documentation showing where the part was originally manufactured or obtained. Without this information it's difficult to determine the authenticity of the part, it's time in service, useful life, status of Airworthiness Directive compliance, as well as many other factors. In fact, in many cases where a part is a component, the only way to determine if it meets airworthiness standards is to perform an overhaul, but even then it may be difficult to determine if all parts used in the component were obtained from a legitimate source. If there is any doubt, it is necessary to reject the component for use on civil aircraft.

In an effort to reduce the risk of unauthorized salvage parts from entering the supply network, whenever a part or component is initially determined to be unserviceable, it should be permanently damaged or destroyed to the extent that it would not be economically feasible to repair and reuse the part.

As an additional consideration, many surplus parts are manufactured for military aircraft use and therefore are not approved for civil aircraft. The military part may appear to be equivalent to a part used on civil aircraft, but often these parts are only manufactured to the military's specifications, which may or may not be sufficient for civil aircraft requirements. On the other hand, regardless of the quality, the part has not been evaluated to establish FAA approval. For example, spark plugs for reciprocating-engine aircraft are manufactured to FAA standards and must be FAA-approved for use in civil aircraft. Military contracts, however, may have been awarded to a manufacturer to produce a number of the same type of spark plugs. While the parts may be identical in material and workmanship, the military part is still not suitable for use in civil aircraft since it has not been monitored by the FAA through the design and manufacturing process.

It should be noted that in some situations, a part that has been manufactured for the military may be subsequently evaluated by the FAA for civil aircraft use. In most cases, if the part has been determined to meet FAA requirements, the individual or organization that requested the evaluation may be granted a Supplemental Type Certificate designating that the parts are approved for civil aircraft use. If an aircraft has these types of parts installed, the purchaser must be able to provide the certifying documentation to support that the part has been granted the proper authorization. In addition, installation of parts approved by an STC requires an FAA Form 337, Major Alteration and Repair, detailing the use of the part on a specific aircraft.

STUDY QUESTIONS

1. List three possible sources where a checklist may be acquired or designed for performing an inspection.

2. What does the term static RPM mean in performing a functional check?

3. List the functional checks that are required on an engine when completing a 100-hour inspection.

4. List the five phases that make up an inspection program on an aircraft.

5. The actual physical inspection of the aircraft is called which phase of the inspection program?

6. How is an aircraft approved for return to service?

7. When is it required to use a part that has been issued a TSO authorization?

Chapter 5
Performing Airworthiness Inspections

Airworthiness inspections, including annuals, 100-hour, progressive, and continuous inspection programs are comprised of similar scope and detail. As such, the conduct of a 100-hour inspection provides insight into the activities that encompass any airworthiness inspection.

This chapter provides an overview of the actions that are taken during the conduct of a typical 100-hour inspection. All aviation personnel should become familiar with these actions to better understand how an inspection is organized and progresses from start to finish. With this understanding, all personnel involved in the inspection process will be able to work together to improve efficiency throughout the inspection, promoting good work relationships through effective communication and cooperation.

PRE-INSPECTION PREPARATION
The 100-hour inspection begins when the owner of an aircraft requests that the inspection be performed on the aircraft. At this time, the work order should be completed listing the desired maintenance to be performed and the owner should present the maintenance records for the aircraft. The pre-inspection phase is very important as it serves to organize the work to be performed. This phase will usually include the following steps.

WORK ORDER COMPLETION
The work order, as previously discussed, is the contract between the shop and the owner of the aircraft concerning the work that is to be performed. It lists the work and serves as a record of parts, supplies and man-hours of labor that are expended on the aircraft. [Figure 5-1]

MAINTENANCE RECORDS
Maintenance records will often tell an inspector a lot about the care and maintenance that an aircraft has had. These records are researched for information concerning the type of oil being used, when spark plugs were last changed, age of the battery, when vacuum system filters were last changed, and engine time since the last overhaul. A very important part of this record research is the notation of compliance with airworthiness directives.

A list of ADs complied with and the method of compliance for each should be drawn up for comparison

Figure 5-1. The work order is the contract between the maintenance shop and the aircraft owner and must be completed in detail prior to performing any work on the aircraft. The work order should specify the extent of work, including the type of servicing that will be included as part of the inspection.

with the FAA's list of ADs that apply to the make and model aircraft, engine(s), propeller(s), and appliances. In some cases a pre-existing AD compliance list may be used as a starting point for compiling the list, but the inspector must determine the actual status of each AD. Any AD found to require action should be planned to be performed at the most appropriate time during the inspection. Additional expenses and time that will be incurred should be determined and discussed with the aircraft owner before performing the maintenance, since it may be outside of their financial resources to make the required repairs at that time.

A list of manufacturer's service letters or bulletins that have been complied with should also be made, as well as doing research into newly released manufacturer's service information that may be incorporated into the inspection.

AIRCRAFT CLEANING
The requirement that the aircraft and engine be cleaned before performing the airworthiness inspection is listed in Appendix D of 14 CFR Part 43. Cleaning of the engine and aircraft is necessary so that a proper inspection of the components can be accomplished. If the source of any fuel, oil, or hydraulic fluid residue can not be determined, it will be necessary to operate the engine or system before beginning the inspection. A

clean engine or aircraft will make the inspection much easier as cracks and discrepancies will not be hidden by dirt and debris. [Figure 5-2]

PARTS AND EQUIPMENT REQUIRED

During the pre-inspection phase, it will become evident that parts or kits required by the maintenance record research, service bulletins and airworthiness directives will be needed. These parts should be ordered as early into the inspection as possible.

Also, each aircraft requires certain types of special shop equipment such as jacks, stands, hydraulic power supplies, external electrical power, and other test equipment. These should be serviced and made readily available in the working area as required.

Small tools and equipment needed include a good source of light, inspection mirrors, a 10X magnifying glass and a supply of cleaning towels. These should also be available in the working area.

Figure 5-2. Initial cleaning is usually accomplished by pressure spray equipment with a subsequent wipe-down of individual areas before each section is inspected. Be sure to follow the aircraft manufacturer's maintenance instructions with regard to types of cleaning materials and methods of application to use on each area of the aircraft.

REMOVAL OF INSPECTION PLATES AND COWLINGS

Before performing a visual inspection, it is necessary to remove or open all inspection plates, access doors, fairings, and cowlings, so the inside of the structure and hidden parts can be inspected. Special care must be taken to keep from losing the screws and plates. In most cases, parts bags should be available to secure the removed hardware to each inspection plate. This makes reinstallation after the inspection much easier. Each inspection plate should also be marked or identified so that they can be reinstalled the same way and in the same location from which they were removed. [Figure 5-3]

REMOVAL OF INTERIOR SEATS, CARPETS, AND UPHOLSTERY

Many aircraft have a requirement to inspect the structure and components of the systems that are located

Figure 5-3. Inspection plates must be removed to gain access to inspect the interior condition of the structure. Not all inspection plates must be removed during an inspection. As long as there is sufficient area to properly inspect the interior, some panels may not have to be removed.

beneath the floor and in the sidewalls of the cabin. This requires removal of many interior parts of the aircraft. Care should be taken to keep from damaging these parts. The seats and upholstery should also be properly stored to keep them from being soiled or damaged. The attachment method of carpets should be carefully noted. Any placards or controls that are removed should be placed in a secure area to keep them from being misplaced.

Determining which plates and fairings to remove is often a problem when inspecting a specific make and model aircraft for the first time. The manufacturer's service manual should be consulted, but the best source of information will be to ask a technician who is experienced on that type aircraft. Cowlings, inspection plates, and all other removed components should be neatly stored on parts racks, with each rack identified by the aircraft registration or customer work order number.

Also during removal of the interior, a detailed inventory of the owner's personal effects should be recorded. These items should be secured to prevent loss or damage. Occasionally the owner or operator will also have items in the cabin that may present a hazard to flight and therefore should be removed. For example, many owners install floor mats or seat covers that while providing added protection to the interior, may present an operational hazard. These items are not usually reinstalled by the mechanic after the inspection, but should be returned to the customer with an explanation as to why they were removed.

INSPECTION REQUIREMENTS

The items to be inspected on the airframe will differ between the various types of aircraft. Persons inspecting an airframe must use the checklist to ensure that they do not overlook any inspection items. The checklist should be placed on a clipboard for access in the shop. As each item is inspected, the checklist item should be initialed by the inspector to indicate its airworthiness acceptance. In addition, maintenance discrepancy reporting forms should be readily available to record any items that need attention once the inspection is complete. As previously discussed, discrepancies should be recorded and corrected by someone that is not involved in the inspection, so as to allow the inspection to progress with as little interruption as possible.

Discrepancy reports should include an area to record the discrepancy, and a separate area for recording corrective actions. Upon completion of the inspection, these forms are used to transfer actions taken during the inspection to the aircraft's permanent maintenance records. Many shops also retain the forms on file with the work order for historical reference.

AIRFRAME INSPECTION

The inspection of the airframe should be done in a logical and systematic manner. A recommended pattern to follow would be to begin the inspection in the interior of the aircraft, then moving to one of the wings, returning to the exterior of the fuselage, moving back to the empennage, then moving forward on the fuselage to the other wing and ending the airframe inspection on the front part of the fuselage and landing gear.

INTERIOR INSPECTION

The inspection of the interior of the aircraft requires that all seats, carpets, upholstery, and inspection panels, requiring removal, have been removed during the pre-inspection phase. A good flashlight, florescent droplight, and an assortment of various size and shape inspection mirrors should be used to properly inspect many difficult to see areas. The items to be inspected may be completed in any sequence that is desired as long as none are overlooked.

A typical inspection procedure of an interior of an aircraft is given as follows:

1. Check the operation and fit of all cabin doors, window stops, latches, locks, hinges, and attaching parts.

2. Check the condition of door and window seals.

3. Inspect the condition of window glass for cracks, crazing, distortion, and overall clarity.

4. Check the seats, upholstery, seat operation mechanism, seat tracks, and stops for proper operation and condition.

5. Check seatbelts for condition, cleanliness, conformity to TSO-C22, security of attachment, and locking of latches. [Figure 5-4]

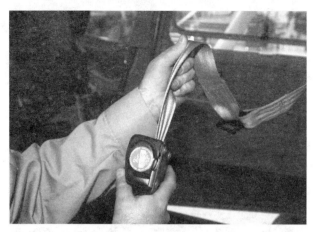

Figure 5-4. Among other things, seat belts should be checked for security of attachment and overall condition. Tattered and frayed edges, and deterioration from sunlight are often causes for rejecting the part as airworthy.

6. Inspect condition of upholstery, carpets, visors, ash trays, and all interior furnishings.

7. Check that the airworthiness certificate is properly displayed and the aircraft registration is in the aircraft.

8. Perform a conformity check of installed equipment by observing if any unusual or different equipment for that type aircraft is installed.

9. Check the operation and condition of fresh air vents, heat and defrost ducts and valves.

10. Inspect the baggage compartment for loose equipment, condition, door operation and locking. [Figure 5-5]

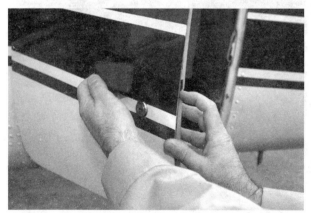

Figure 5-5. Baggage compartments undergo abuse, so take a close look for damage to seals and locking mechanisms.

11. Inspect the ELT for proper installation, battery replacement date, antennae connection condition, cable routing, and operation. Perform 12 month ELT test when required by 14 CFR Part 91.207.

12. Inspect rudder pedals and attaching parts for operation, condition, and security of attachment.

13. Inspect brake master cylinders for operation, fluid level, attachment, and plumbing.

14. Check control yokes, slides, chains, cables, pulleys and turnbuckles for security, operation, safety, chafing, freedom of movement, rotation, and general condition. [Figure 5-6]

Figure 5-6. A close look under the instrument panel is required to check the control yoke operation. Push, pull, and turn the control yoke while inspecting to check for adequate clearance from wire bundles and other obstructions that may interfere with proper operation.

15. Inspect operation of the trim operating mechanisms, linkages, indicators, cables and pulleys. [Figure 5-7]

Figure 5-7. Control cables must be closely examined. Often a defect is not easily seen. To detect frayed strands, run a cotton cloth along the length of the cable. If strands are frayed, the cloth will snag without injuring your hand.

16. Check the manually operated flap system for operation, locking, binding, security of attachment, and indicators for proper operation and position.

17. Check fuel selector and shut off valves for leaks, binding, detent feel, placarding, and operation.

18. Inspect fuel system plumbing for chafing, damage, leaks, security, and routing.

19. Check primer for leakage, operation, sticking, and locking.

20. Inspect the magnetic compass for leakage, fluid level, condition, mounting, and calibration on the compass correction card. [Figure 5-8]

Figure 5-8. Magnetic compasses should not only be checked for operation, but to make sure the compass correction card is installed and accurate.

21. Inspect all plumbing and electrical wiring behind the instrument panel for routing, chafing, security of attachment, and leakage. [Figure 5-9]

Figure 5-9. Inspecting behind the panel can be complicated but it is an important part of the inspection. All wiring and plumbing must be properly secured.

22. Inspect vacuum system filters and screens for cleanliness, security, and attachment of hoses and lines.

23. Check all instruments for proper mounting, condition (if practical), for proper operation, operating limit marking in accordance with the aircraft TCDS, and attachment of wires and hoses.

24. Check instrument panel shock mounts and bonding straps for condition and movement of the panel.

25. Check engine controls for freedom of movement, travel, operation, and condition.

26. Check for required placarding and marking of controls, switches and instruments.

27. Check the operation of all miscellaneous knobs, and controls mounted on the instrument panel and in the cabin.

28. Check all instrument and cabin lights for operation and condition.

29. Inspect all fuses, circuit breakers, switches, and wiring for condition, operation, marking, and attachment.

30. Inspect the battery box, vents, solenoids, cables, and wiring for improper installation, operation, and general condition.

31. Check the battery for water level and proper state of charge.

32. Inspect the interior of the tail cone for general condition, corrosion, cracking, cable routing, pulley operation, and loose objects.

WING INSPECTION

1. Inspect external wing structure or fabric for general condition, deterioration, damage and corrosion.

2. Inspect the internal structure for corrosion, damage, and general condition.

3. Inspect wing attachments for security.

4. Inspect external struts for condition and attachment.

5. Check the pitot tube for attachment, heating, and plumbing.

6. Check stall warning switches or reeds for proper operation.

7. Check navigation and landing lights for operation, and security of mounting.

8. Inspect ailerons for attachment, operation, and condition. [Figure 5-10]

9. Check flaps for operation, condition, and security of attachment.

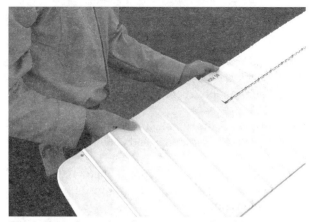

Figure 5-10. Control surface movement is critical because often these surfaces are balanced. Especially check for hinge wear and free-play.

10. Check aileron control system cables, pulleys, fairleads, push-pull rods, bearings, bellcranks, turnbuckles, and stops for proper operation, condition, and safetied attachment.

11. Check flap operating mechanisms for operation, lubrication, security of attachment, and freedom of movement.

12. Inspect the trim tab system for operation, attachment, and general condition.

13. Inspect fuel tanks, fuel caps, vents, plumbing, and quantity indicating systems for leakage, proper operation, and marking of fuel filler openings.

14. Check fuel sumps and screens for cleanliness, and contamination.

15. Check condition of bonding straps and static discharge wicks. [Figure 5-11]

Figure 5-11. Bonding straps should be checked for security and corrosion. Either can cause high electrical resistance that may prevent an easy flow of current from the adjacent structure to the control surface.

FUSELAGE INSPECTION

1. Inspect external wing skin or fabric for general condition, deterioration, damage, and corrosion.

2. Check the static ports for cleanliness and freedom from obstructions.

3. Inspect radio antennas for proper operation, attachment, mounting, and condition.

4. Inspect internal parts through appropriate inspection panels for condition, attachment, and operation as applicable.

5. Inspect the cabin entrance step and operating mechanism for condition and proper operation.

EMPENNAGE INSPECTION

1. Inspect the horizontal stabilizer for condition and security of attachment.

2. Inspect the elevator and hinges for condition, freedom of movement, travel, and security of attachment.

3. Inspect the elevator trim tab for condition, security of attachment free play and proper operation.

4. Inspect the vertical stabilizer for condition and security of attachment.

5. Inspect the rudders for condition, freedom of movement, travel and security of attachment.

6. Inspect anti-collision beacons for condition and security.

7. Inspect navigation antenna for proper attachment and condition. Especially look for seal condition and proper electrical grounding.

LANDING GEAR INSPECTION

1. Raise the aircraft so the landing gear is clear of the floor by jacking or hoisting.

2. Remove the wheels, inspect and repack the bearings, inspect wheels and tires, and check for proper tire inflation pressures.

3. Inspect brake linings, discs, clips, and wheel cylinders for wear, leakage, and condition.

4. Inspect axle and install wheel and brakes on axle and safety.

5. Deflate shock struts and check fluid level as required, and inflate struts to recommended pressure.

6. Inspect rudder shock cords for condition and age.

7. Inspect tail wheel assembly and springs (when installed) for condition, security of attachment, and operation of steering mechanism.

8. Inspect shimmy damper for security of attachment, leakage, fluid level, and for excessive wear in the attachment.

9. Inspect nose steering mechanism for wear, security of attachment, freedom of operation, condition, excessive wear, and centering mechanism for operation.

10. Check torque links or scissors for condition, wear, cracks, excessive play, and condition.

11. Inspect landing gear struts for security of attachment, leakage, cleanliness, and general condition.

12. Check landing gear retraction and extension mechanism for leakage, wear, damage, security of attachment, cleanliness, and general condition.

13. Check brake and hydraulic hoses and lines for leakage, chafing, proper support, damage, age hardening, and general condition.

14. Check electrical switches and wiring for cleanliness, chafing, proper support, and general condition.

15. Inspect landing gear doors, linkages, hinges and operating mechanisms for wear, damage, distortion, cleanliness, fit, security of attachment, and general condition.

16. Retractable landing gear operational check procedures:

   a. Jack aircraft clear of the floor.

   b. Check the retraction safety switch for proper operation and adjustment using the procedures specified in the service manual.

   c. Disconnect appropriate doors and linkages and secure out of the way of the gear operation.

   d. Operate retraction system until the down locking mechanism is released. Check gear struts, linkages, cylinders, and rods for excessive clearances and wear.

   e. After checking for wear and clearances, continue to retract the gear and observe the gear for proper operation, binding, chafing, operation of the uplocks and electrical switches.

f. While the gear is in the retracted position, check the up-lock tension and clearances, operation of the landing gear up indicating lights, adjustment and operation of the throttle warning switches, lights, and horn.

g. Extend the landing gear while observing the extension mechanism and gear linkages for proper operation, binding, chafing, and movement.

h. Check the down-lock for proper operation, tension, and clearance, indicating lights and switches for adjustment and operation.

i. Check the down-lock indicating lights and switches for adjustment and operation.

j. Reconnect all the doors and linkages and safety.

k. Retract the landing gear. Observe the operation of the doors and linkages. Check doors for fit, clearances, and tension.

l. Extend the landing gear using the emergency extension mechanism and check for operation, down-lock engagement and indicating lights for proper operation.

m. Retract and extend the landing gear by the normal system to ensure proper operation.

n. Remove the aircraft from the jacks and adjust the strut inflation as necessary for proper strut extension.

ENGINE INSPECTION

The inspection of the engine should be as extensive as necessary to ensure that the engine is in an airworthy condition. The engine should be cleaned and its hoses, plumbing lines, and electrical wiring should be neatly clamped and supported from chaffing and to avoid heat damage from the exhaust system.

The inspection of the engine may require some disassembly to perform a large number of the inspection items. A planned sequence should be used in addition to the checklist to make sure that no inspection details are omitted.

INTERNAL ENGINE CONDITION

The internal condition of a reciprocating engine is determined by checking the compression of the cylinders and inspecting the oil screen to see if there are any metal particles adhering to it that have been strained out of the oil. The procedures for checking the cylinder compression and oil screen are as follows:

CYLINDER COMPRESSION

The differential pressure compression tester is the most satisfactory method of checking the cylinders to see that the valves and rings are not leaking excessively. Usually the top spark plugs and the ignition leads on the bottom plugs are removed to prevent accidental firing of the cylinders when the propeller is rotated by hand.

The spark plug adapter for the tester is then inserted into the number one cylinder spark plug hole and tightened. A source of compressed air is the connected to the tester. This air source should have a capacity in excess of 80 PSI. The air pressure flowing through the orifice in the tester should be adjusted to the pressure as specified in the service manual, usually either 20 PSI or 80 PSI, depending on the engine being tested.

The next step is to place the piston on either bottom center or top center of the compression stroke as specified by the manufacturer. Slowly open the air valve while standing clear of the propeller, or have another person hold the propeller stationary as the valve is opened. [Figure 5-12]

Figure 5-12. For added safety, it is better for two people to perform a compression check. One person operates the compression tester, while the other holds the propeller to prevent it from swinging around when air is added to the cylinder.

Record the compression value of each cylinder on the checklist. Using the firing order of the engine, check all cylinders in sequence. Caution should be taken to protect against the rapid movement of the propeller if the air valve is opened rapidly.

All the cylinders should be approximately equal to each other in compression and each cylinder should be above 75% of the applied air pressure or as specified by the engine manufacturer. If excessive leakage is noted, attempt to determine the cause of the leakage. This can be done by listening to determine if the air is escaping out of the exhaust pipe, air intake, or through the crankcase breather. This will help determine what maintenance will be required to repair the cylinder leakage.

OIL SCREEN CHECK

The removal of the oil screen or oil filter is required to determine if the engine is having excessive and destructive wear or deterioration. This is determined by checking to see if any metal particles are present on the screen and in the screen housing. Oil filters that are becoming popular on today's engines must be cut open and inspected. If metal particles are found, the source of the metal will have to be determined and a decision made as to whether the engine is airworthy.

IGNITION SYSTEM CHECKS

The spark plugs should be removed and stored in a rack that is labeled for each cylinder. As each plug is removed, the electrode end should be examined for possible combustion deposits. This will often display the internal condition of the cylinder, operation of the fuel system, and the way the pilot is operating the engine. The plugs should then be cleaned, pressure tested, and gapped. Upon installation, new spark plug gaskets should be used and the plug torqued to the proper value.

Ignition leads should be checked for general condition, proper routing, cleanliness, condition of the plug ends, security, chafing, and heat damage.

The magnetos should be inspected in accordance with the particular manufacturer's recommendations of timing, breaker point condition, lubrication, security of mounting, internal oil leakage, lead attachment, and general condition. The model number and part number should be carefully checked against the airworthiness directives and service bulletins to see if any directives or bulletins apply to them. The propeller should be rotated to ensure that the impulse couplings (if installed) are functioning properly.

EXHAUST SYSTEM INSPECTION

The exhaust system should be checked for leakage, security of mounting, cracks, warpage, and general condition. The heat shroud around the mufflers should be removed and the muffler carefully checked for leakage, discoloration, cracks, and general condition. A flashlight and a mirror should be used to check the inside of the muffler for loose or missing flame arrestors and baffles. The muffler should be checked against the airworthiness directives to see if any directives apply to it. The flexible air ducts or hoses should be checked for condition and security. If a turbo-supercharger is installed it should be inspected in accordance with the manufacturer's recommendations.

ENGINE CONTROLS

The throttle, carburetor heat, mixture, cowl flap, oil cooler, propeller and heat controls should be checked for routing, chafing, security, safety, excessive wear, damage, and general condition. Each control should be operationally checked for full travel, freedom, binding, and proper operation. The throttle and mixture linkages should be checked for excessive wear and proper safety. The carburetor heat box and valve should be checked for wear and damage.

GENERAL ENGINE INSPECTION

The engine compartment should be checked for evidence of fuel, oil, and hydraulic leaks and the source of any leaks determined. All fuel, oil and hydraulic hoses should be checked for condition, age hardening, chafing, security, routing, and general condition. The cooling baffles and seals should be checked for cracks, security, mounting, and general condition. Studs and nuts should be checked for obvious defects and evidence of looseness. The intake system should be checked for security of attachment and for signs of leakage. The carburetor and fuel pump should be checked for security of attachment, safety, general condition, and leakage. The cylinders should be checked for broken fins, evidence of leakage, and general condition. Periodically, the cylinder hold down bolt torque should also be checked. Special attention should be given to the hold down flange areas of the crankcase to look for cracks or signs of leakage. [Figure 5-13 and 5-14]

The oil cooler should be inspected for leakage, security of attachment, and general condition. The engine mount and vibration dampeners and mounts should be checked for cracks, corrosion, damage, security of attachment, deterioration, and general condition. All accessories should be checked for security of mounting, general condition and obvious defects. The dust cover should be removed from the starters and generators and the condition of the brushes and commutator checked. All electrical wiring and bundles should be checked for proper security, routing, and general condition. Inspect the firewall for leakage, damage, and general condition. Check the entire crankcase for cracks, leakage, and general condition. Inspect the breather tube and lines for obstruction, routing, security, and general condition. Generator and Alternator drive belts should be checked for tension, deterioration, and general condition. The cowling should be inspected for cracks, condition of fasteners, damage, and general condition.

PROPELLER INSPECTION

The inspection of the propeller will require that the propeller spinner be removed so that the hub and mounting bolts can be inspected. The hub should be checked for cracks, leakage of grease and oil, corrosion, and general condition. The propeller mounting bolts should be checked for proper torque and safety. [Figure 5-15]

The blades should be checked for nicks, deep scratches, corrosion, cracks, and obvious damage. The

ENGINE GROUP	50	100	200	SPL INSP
CAUTION — Ground Magneto Primary Circuit Before Working on the Engine				
1. Engine: Wash, check for security of accessories		✓		
2. Cowling: Wash, check for cracks, evidence of abrasion and wear			✓	
3. Induction Air Filter: Clean				6
4. Induction Manifold: Check connections for condition		✓		
5. Engine Oil Pressure System: Check for leaks, bends, cracks and security		✓		
6. Engine Oil Filter: Change oil filter element and Inspect adadapters		✓		
7. Engine Oil: Change		✓		
8. Engine Oil Separator: Inspect and clean element. Refer to Service Chart				6
9. Engine Compartment: Visually check for condition, oil leaks, fuel leaks, etc.		✓		
10. Engine Controls: Check travel and security		✓		
11. Engine Wire Bundle: Check for condition and security		✓		
12. Engine Mounts: Check for condition and security		✓		
13. Engine Compartment Hoses: Fuel (check fuel lines under pressure), oil vacuum, etc. Check deterioration, leaks, discoloration, bleaching, and rubber hoses for stiffness	✓			
14. Cylinder Compression: Refer to Manufacturer's Service Bulletin m73-19		✓		
15. Engine Cylinders, Rocker Box Covers and Push Rod Housing: Check for fin damage, cracks, oil leakage, security of attachment and general condition		✓		
16. Crankcase, Oil Sump, and Accessory Section: Inspect for cracks and evidence of oil leakage. Check bolts and nuts for looseness and retorque as necessary			✓	
17. Plugs: Clean and rotate (top right to bottom left, to top right)		✓		
18. Ignition Cables: Check condition and security		✓		
19. Magneto: Check timing, breaker gap and security				14
20. Alternator: Check brushes, leads, bearings and slip rings				7
21. Starter: Check brushes, commutator and electrical connections		✓		
22. Propeller Governor: Check for oil leaks, condition and security			✓	
23. Pumps-Fuel, Vacuum and Autopilot: Check for leaks, condition and security		✓		
24. Turbocharger: Check for condition, bulges, warps and security		✓		
25. Engine Exhaust System: Check for security, cracks, bellows and spring tension	✓			
26. Engine Exhaust System: Check for security, cracks, and spring tension, inspect slip join seals				
27. Waste Gate Valve, Variable Absolute Pressure Controller and Check for condition and security. Visually check springs and				
28. Manifold Pressure Relief Valve: Visually check for observation and proper operation				
29. Engine Oil Screen: Check for removal (refer to expanded para				
30. Engine Compartment Fire Extinguisher: Check system pressu				

Figure 5-13. Sample page of a service manual showing the engine equipment inspection requirements.

Figure 5-14. The smallest item, if overlooked during an airworthiness inspection, could cause some of the biggest problems.

Figure 5-15. The propeller blades and hub assembly must be checked for play, cracks, and corrosion.

spinner and backplate should be checked for cracks and security of attachment. On a controllable-pitch propeller, the blades should be checked for any airworthiness directives that may apply to them. The condition of the paint on the blades should be checked and repainted, if necessary. [Figure 5-16]

Figure 5-16. Propeller nicks and scratches must be properly removed and blended to avoid in-flight blade failures.

ELECTRONIC INSTALLATIONS

The inspection of the radios and electronic installations can be conducted during the inspection of the areas in which they are located, or inspected as an independent group depending upon the operating procedure of each individual shop.

The electronic equipment that is installed should be checked against the equipment list and weight and balance data to ensure that it has been properly recorded in the maintenance records. The equipment should be checked for security of attachment, improper installation procedures, bonding, condition of shock mounts, and general condition. The bonding and shielding of all wiring and equipment should be checked for improper installation and poor condition. [Figure 5-17]

The emergency locator transmitter (ELT) should be checked for proper installation, battery replacement date, condition of the antenna and wiring. The unit

Figure 5-17. Check mounting and security of all electronic component installations.

should also be checked for the proper operation of the G-switch.

The antenna should be checked for proper installation, loose mounting, grounding, and general condition.

SERVICE AND REPAIR PHASE

The necessary servicing and repair needed to return the aircraft to service as airworthy should be completed as a separate function from the actual inspection. Only those service functions that can be easily included with inspection items may be performed during the inspection phase—and then only if they do not upset the inspection procedure.

The requirements of the service manual for each aircraft model should be followed to determine the items that are to be serviced, type of service required, method of application, time interval between each service, and products to be used to complete the servicing.

The servicing required on the airframe consists of the lubrication of the control system moving parts, replacement or cleaning of the vacuum system filters, draining of the fuel sumps and gascolator (if installed). Additional items include cleaning the fuel screens and filters, testing the charge and condition of the battery, cleaning the battery and battery compartments, servicing the battery sump, drains and vent system. [Figure 5-18]

The servicing of the landing gear and brake system consists of adding fluid and air to the struts, lubrication of the landing gear, lubrication and cleaning of the wheel bearings, inflation of the tires, adding fluid to the brake and hydraulic reservoir, adding fluid to the shimmy damper, and the cleaning of gear switches and rollers.

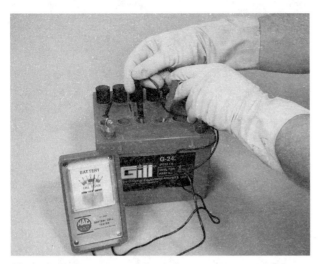

Figure 5-18. Battery servicing is important to control corrosion and ensure dependable starting power.

Servicing of the engine and propeller consists of adding the correct type and amount of oil to the crankcase, cleaning or replacement of the carburetor air intake filter, cleaning or replacement of the oil filter or screens, cleaning and draining of the carburetor, fuel system sumps and screens, lubrication of the control linkages, lubrication of the propeller, checking and adding nitrogen to the propeller accumulator, filing of minor nicks and scratches on the propeller blades, and repainting of the propeller face and tips.

The repair phase consists of repairing the discrepancies that were discovered during the look phase of the inspection. This phase can also be used to comply with airworthiness directive and service bulletin requirements that are due or will become due prior to the next scheduled inspection of the aircraft.

POST INSPECTION

The post inspection phase consists of preparing the aircraft for its return to service. This phase should be accomplished with a great eye for small details as the owner of the aircraft often judges the quality of the inspection by the way the aircraft looks and runs after the inspection is complete.

INSTALLATION OF INTERIOR AND INSPECTION PANELS

The installation of the interior, carpets, upholstery, and seats should be done with great care and attention to detail. The original fasteners should be used to attach the upholstery and contact cement or velcro tapes can be used to hold carpets in their proper place. The seat belts should be neatly arranged and the controls checked for freedom of movement.

Inspection panels and fairings should be installed in their proper position using new hardware to replace damaged or worn out screws and nuts. The screws should be installed secure enough to properly hold the panel but not so tight as to make removal nearly impossible. Remember, you may be the one that has to remove them at the next inspection.

CLEANLINESS OF THE AIRCRAFT

The cleanliness of the aircraft, both interior and exterior may be one of the few obvious signs to the aircraft owner that anything was accomplished on the aircraft for the several hundred dollars that the inspection has cost. It is very important that the aircraft and engine be thoroughly cleaned and neat in appearance. [Figure 5-19]

Figure 5-19. Solvent spraying equipment is often used for engine cleaning, followed by hand wiping of individual components.

The engine compartment should be washed with a suitable cleaning solvent using an air pressure cleaning gun to remove all oil and dirt residue.

The interior should be vacuumed and cleaned, the instrument glass and panel dusted and cleaned. All the interior windows cleaned and ashtrays emptied. All knobs and control switches cleaned. All of the miscellaneous articles located in the cabin and baggage compartment should be secured and neatly stowed away.

The airframe exterior should be washed and cleaned again upon completion of the inspection. The belly should be thoroughly cleaned of all oil and exhaust residue. The windows should be cleaned and protected with an approved static free wax. Exposed portions of the landing gear struts should be cleaned and wiped with an approved lubricant. [Figure 5-20]

Figure 5-20. Cleaning the aircraft prior to approving it for return to service is important, as often it is the only obvious change an aircraft owner will detect after an inspection.

FUNCTIONAL CHECKS

The functional checks required after an inspection has been completed will vary from one type of aircraft to another, but will consist of an operational check of almost every system installed in the aircraft to ensure they will perform properly.

The airframe systems to be checked consist of: landing and navigation lights, anti-collision lights or strobes, instrument lights, wing flap operation, flight control systems, radio and navigation equipment where practical, instrument operation where practical, fuel selector valve and system, stall warning system, heating and ventilating systems, and pitot heat operation. [Figure 5-21]

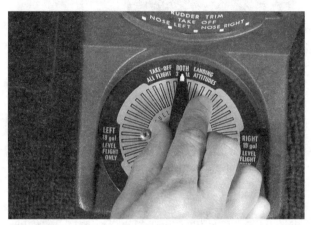

Figure 5-21. A functional check of each of the aircraft's systems helps to avoid in-flight problems.

As previously discussed, the engine and propellers should operate properly, according to the manufacturer's recommendations. 14 CFR Part 43.15 requires that the engine be operated to determine satisfactory operation in accordance with the manufacturer's recommendation of power output (both static and idle RPM), magnetos, fuel and oil pressure, and cylinder and oil temperature.

The functional checks on the engine consist of a fuel pressure check to ensure that none of the fuel system is leaking, engine run-up to check the operation of the magnetos, propeller, carburetor heat, idle speed and idle mixture, maximum static RPM, fuel and oil pressures, cylinder and oil temperature, hydraulic system pressure, generator or alternator operations, instrument vacuum pressure, de-icing or anti-icing system operation. After engine shutdown a check should be made for evidence of fluid leakage in the engine compartment. [Figure 5-22]

RETURN TO SERVICE PROCEDURES

The return to service phase is the completion of the proper entries in the aircraft and maintenance records of all the work performed on the aircraft.

The requirement for the return to service entry for a 100-hour inspection is found in 14 CFR Part 43.11 and

Figure 5-22. Functional checks may also include actual flight testing of the aircraft.

consists of the following information: type of inspection, date of the inspection, aircraft time in service, certification statement, signature, and the certificate number. An entry commonly in use is as follows:

Sample Entry

May 30, 1992   Total Time: 488 Hours

I certify that this aircraft (or engine) has been inspected in accordance with a 100-hour inspection and was determined to be in airworthy condition.

Harold B. Nelson
A&P No. 1607438

The common practice is to make an entry in the airframe record and another entry in the engine and propeller record for the return to service after the 100-hour inspection has been completed. Annual and progressive inspections however, are usually only indicated in the airframe record.

When repair work or airworthiness directives have been accomplished, it is common practice to include these items in a paragraph between the date and time in service and the inspection certification part of the entry. An entry commonly in use is as follows:

Combination Sample Entry

May 30, 1992   Total Time: 488 Hours

Battery replaced, left main gear tire replaced, new brake lining installed on both main gear, AD 76-03-99, revision date, August 14, 1977, complied with by replacing the fuel selector in accordance with Paragraph B, Service bulletin SE 78-10 complied with.

I certify that this aircraft has been inspected in accordance with a 100-hour inspection and was determined to be in airworthy condition.

John Lawson
A&P No. 1607438

STUDY QUESTIONS

1. Must an airworthiness directive that is due be complied with before a 100-hour inspection can be approved for return to service?

2. Must service bulletins on most small aircraft be complied with before the aircraft can be approved for return to service?

3. List the things you would inspect on the seatbelts installed in an aircraft.

4. What two certificates must be in the aircraft at all times?

5. List the inspection requirements of the ELT.

6. List the inspection requirements for the aircraft battery.

7. List the inspection requirements for an operational check of the retractable landing gear.

8. What are two checks that are accomplished to determine the internal condition of the engine?

9. List the inspection requirements for a magneto during a 100-hour inspection.

Chapter 6

Major Repairs and Alterations

Within 14 CFR Part 43 Appendix A, the FAA outlines major repairs and alterations for airframes, engines, propellers, and other accessories. It is the mechanic who must make the decision regarding whether or not a repair or alteration is major or minor. Appendix A provides a useful guide for mechanics in making these determinations. Frequently however, the specific repair or alteration may not be listed in the regulation. In such cases, the mechanic must first contact the manufacturer and then the local FAA office for guidance. When all other avenues have been exhausted, a mechanic must ask three questions:

1. Would the repair or alteration prevent continued safety of flight?

2. Would the repair prevent safe landings?

3. Would the repair affect the safety of the crew and passengers in an adverse manner?

A "yes" to any of these questions indicates that the repair or alteration is considered major. A major repair is defined as a repair that if done improperly, might appreciably affect weight, balance, structural strength, performance, powerplant operation, flight characteristics, or other qualities affecting airworthiness. A major repair may also be a repair that is not done in accordance with accepted practices or cannot be done by elementary operations. Repairs of this type must always return the affected item back to the original type design rendering it airworthy.

Accordingly, a major alteration is an alteration not listed in the aircraft, engine, or propeller specifications that might appreciably affect weight, balance, structural strength, performance, powerplant operation, flight characteristics, or other qualities affecting airworthiness. A major alteration may also be one that is not done in accordance with accepted practices or cannot be done by elementary operations. It is a change to the original type design.

FORM 337 REQUIREMENTS

Any time a major repair or major alteration is performed, it must be returned to service by the use of an FAA Form 337. This form, titled Major Repair and Alteration, provides the owner with a record of major repairs and alterations performed on their aircraft's airframe, engine, propeller, or accessories. It also provides the FAA with a form to include in the aircraft records maintained by the FAA Aircraft Registration Branch. [Figure 6-1 shown on pages 6-3 and 6-4]

The Form 337 is typically completed by the technician performing the repair or alteration. It records the specific component affected and the method by which it was repaired or altered. The form and its required signatures assure that the airframe, or other aircraft components in question, have been repaired or altered in a manner consistent with maintaining original airworthiness as required by the airworthiness certificate. Additionally, the Form 337 provides a means for other aircraft owners, operators, and technicians to research alterations and repairs previously performed. This research can aid in the approval process for others desiring to utilize similar repair or alteration techniques and procedures.

FAA APPROVALS

The FAA requires a mechanic to use approved data when performing a major repair or alteration as required by 14 CFR part 65.95, 121.378, 135.437, and 145.51. Questions regarding the ability to use specific information as approved information should be directed to the local FAA office. Approved data can come from a variety of sources including

Type Certificate Data and Specifications (TCDS)

Supplemental Type Certificate (STC)

Airworthiness Directive (AD)

Technical Standard Order (TSO) Authorization (installation data must come from somewhere else such as an STC, TCDS, or AD)

Parts Manufacturer Authorization (PMA) (approved for specific application, but may require an STC for installation)

Delegated Option Authorization (DOA)

Appliance Manufacturer's Manuals

Designated Alteration Station (DAS)

Designated Engineering Representative (DER)

FAA Approved Data

SFAR 36 Repair Data

Advisory Circular (AC) 43.13-1B provided:

- It is appropriate to the product being repaired or altered,

- It is directly applicable to the repair or alteration, and

- It is not contrary to manufacturer's data

FIELD APPROVAL

Any time approved information is not available for a specific repair or alteration, the technician must seek alternate approval from the FAA. This comes in the form of a field approval, which is an approval by the FAA Airworthiness Inspector by:

Examination of acceptable data which is then documented as FAA-approved data

Examination by physical inspection, demonstration, or testing of the repair or alteration

Examination of data for duplication of repair or alteration on an identical make and model by the original modifier.

Approvals of this kind are not FAA regulation, but rather an FAA policy, therefore an approval for the procedure is not necessarily guaranteed and is completely dependent upon the inspector. It is entirely acceptable to seek a field approval from a second inspector if the repair or alteration proposal is denied by the initial inspector.

It is a good policy to seek a field approval prior to beginning a repair or alteration on an aircraft in the event the approval cannot be granted. Technicians can contact the local FAA Airworthiness Inspector in order to discuss the type of information and data the inspector will require for the field approval. This may include drawings, photographs, manuals, bulletins, and a cover letter accurately describing the repair or alteration. Additionally, the inspector may desire Instructions for Continued Airworthiness (ICA) which convey instructions to other technicians on how to properly maintain an alteration. Information on creating an ICA is included in the Handbook Bulletin for Airworthiness (HBAW) 98-18, *Checklist for Instructions for Continued Airworthiness for Major Alterations Approved Under the Field Approval Process.*

There are several types of repairs and alterations that cannot be authorized by a field approval. When a field approval is not able to be granted, the technician must seek an STC. STCs are required for increases in gross weight, major changes in center of gravity ranges, repairs or modifications that affect structural integrity, flight, or ground handling, changes to control surface travel, control surface dimensions, or aircraft dimensions, changes to engine cooling, fuel vents, fire extinguishing systems, and a variety of other installations that constitute a major change to a type design. Incomplete, or partial repairs and alterations, or procedures requiring engineering approval, also typically require an STC.

COMPLETION OF THE FORM 337

The Form 337 must be filled out and filed with the owner and FAA as specified in 14 CFR Part 43 Appendix B and the current version of Advisory Circular (AC) 43.9-1G. A copy of this advisory circular is included in the appendices of this book. Information that is required on the form includes the aircraft make, model, serial number, nationality and registration mark, and owner information. The technician making the repair must also include information about the airframe, powerplant, propeller, or appliance, and a description of the repair and alteration as well as the data used to perform the procedure.

When marking the form, it is important to identify which component is affected. For example, if an anti-collision light is installed on an aircraft, the airframe is altered, but not the component that was installed. Therefore, only an airframe major alteration would be recorded on the form unless the anti-collision light was modified from its original design.

In order for the Form 337 to be considered complete, the technician performing the repair/alteration must sign the conformity statement, and an approval for return to service must be given by the FAA or a person authorized by the FAA. If the repair or alteration is accomplished using approved data, is performed in accordance with applicable regulations, and found to conform to all airworthiness standards, the return to service authorization can be given by the manufacturer of the airframe, engine, propeller, or accessory. Approval for return to service can also be granted by a repair station, an A&P Mechanic holding an Inspection Authorization (IA), a person approved by Transport Canada Airworthiness Group, or any other person specifically authorized by the FAA. For repairs or alterations made with acceptable data or unapproved data, a field approval, including the return to service approval, must be made by an FAA Inspector or FAA designee.

On the back of the Form 337, space is provided to describe, clearly and concisely, the repair or alteration performed and the precise location of the repair or

US Department of Transportation
Federal Aviation Administration

MAJOR REPAIR AND ALTERATION
(Airframe, Powerplant, Propeller, or Appliance)

Form Approved
OMB No. 2120-0020

For FAA Use Only
Office Identification

INSTRUCTIONS: Print or type all entries. See FAR 43.9, FAR 43 Appendix B, and AC 43.9-1 (or subsequent revision thereof) for instructions and disposition of this form. This report is required by law (49 U.S.C. 1421). Failure to report can result in civil penalty not to exceed $1,000 for each such violation (Section 901 Federal Aviation Act of 1958).

1. Aircraft	Make: Cessna	Model: 172 K
	Serial No.: 12345678	Nationality and Registration Mark: N 00110

2. Owner	Name (As shown on registration certificate): John Doe	Address (As shown on registration certificate): Box 00 Anytown, WY

3. For FAA Use Only

4. Unit Identification | 5. Type

Unit	Make	Model	Serial No.	Repair	Alteration
AIRFRAME	—————— (As described in Item 1 above) ——————			X	
POWERPLANT					
PROPELLER					
APPLIANCE	Type:				
	Manufacturer:				

6. Conformity Statement

A. Agency's Name and Address	B. Kind of Agency	C. Certificate No.
Sam Jones RR 3 Somewhere, USA	U.S. Certificated Mechanic Foreign Certificated Mechanic Certificated Repair Station Manufacturer	A&P 000123456

D. I certify that the repair and/or alteration made to the unit(s) identified in item 4 above and described on the reverse or attachments hereto have been made in accordance with the requirements of Part 43 of the U.S. Federal Aviation Regulations and that the information furnished herin is true and correct to the best of my knowledge.

Date	Signature of Authorized Individual
June 0, 0000	*Sam Jones*

7. Approval for Return To Service

Pursuant to the authority given persons specified below, the unit identified in item 4 was inspected in the manner prescribed by the Administrator of the Federal Aviation Administration and is ☒ APPROVED ☐ REJECTED

BY	FAA Flt. Standards Inspector	Manufacturer	X	Inspection Authorization	Other (Specify)
	FAA Designee	Repair Station		Person Approved by Transport Canada Airworthiness Group	

Date of Approval or Rejection	Certificate or Designation No.	Signature of Authorized Individual
June 0, 0000	00110001 IA	*James R. Roberts*

FAA Form 337 (12-88) AFS Electronic Forms System

Figure 6-1. FAA Form 337

NOTICE

Weight and balance or operating limitation changes shall be entered in the appropriate aircraft record. An alteration must be compatible with all previous alterations to assure continued conformity with the applicable airworthiness requirements.

8. Description of Work Accomplished
   (If more space is required, attach additional sheets. Identify with aircraft nationality and registration mark and date work completed.)

1. Replace the firewall with a new firewall in accordance with Cessna structural repair manual, para. 3, figure 18, and procedures and practices outline in section 3, Chapter 2 of AC 43.13–1A.
----------------- end -------------

☐ Additional Sheets Are Attached

AFS Electronic Forms System

alteration. It should be noted that approved information and instructions were used as the basis for the procedure and that they were followed in making the repair/alteration. These instructions must be specifically identified. The FAA inspector, or other authorized person, can only approve the repair or alteration for return to service if approved data and instructions were used to perform the repair and the work was performed in an approved manner.

DISPOSITION, RETENTION, AND TRANSFER OF THE FORM 337

Two copies of the Form 337 must be completed and signed. The original copy should be provided to the aircraft owner for placement in the aircraft maintenance records. Repair records must be retained for one year while alteration records must be retained for the life of the aircraft and transferred to the new owner if the aircraft is sold. The second copy must be sent to the local FAA office within 48 hours of the approval for return to service of the aircraft, engine, propeller, or appliance that was affected. Additionally, the installation of extended-range fuel tanks in the passenger or baggage compartments requires a third copy of a Form 337. The third copy must be maintained on board the aircraft as specified in 14 CFR Part 91.417.

According to Appendix B of 14 CFR Part 43, a signed copy of a repair work order may be given to the owner in lieu of a Form 337. This is only valid, however, for repair stations performing a major repair. In this case, it is necessary for the repair station to maintain a copy of the work order in their records for at least two years from the date of approval for return to service. In addition to the signed work order, the repair station must also provide the aircraft owner with a signed maintenance release. The release should be retained in the aircraft's permanent maintenance records until the work is repeated or superceded, or for at least one year after the work is completed.

STUDY QUESTIONS

1. What actions can airframe and powerplant mechanics perform with regard to major alterations and major repairs?

2. Must an FAA form 337 be completed after an engine is exchanged for another make and model engine that is approved for installation as indicated in the TCDS?

3. When an FAA Form 337 is required for a major alteration or repair, how many forms are required to be filled out?

4. Within how many hours must the Form 337 be submitted to the FAA once an aircraft has been approved for return to service after a major alteration or major repair?

Chapter 7
Maintenance Records

Historical data regarding the care and maintenance of an aircraft is crucial for safety and to maintain the aircraft's maximum value. Maintenance history is recorded and tracked in various ways. It may be contained in hardcopy logbooks, or, as has become common in recent years, they may be maintained electronically in computerized logbooks. Due to the large variety of electronic logbook programs that are available, this text focuses only on the methods for retaining and recording maintenance history in hardcopy logbooks. For information regarding computerized maintenance tracking systems, consult the developer's instructions for the specific product.

OWNERS' RESPONSIBILITIES
The owner or operator is responsible for holding and maintaining the maintenance records for their aircraft. They are required to present those records to maintenance personnel and ensure that appropriate entries are made to indicate the aircraft has been released for service after maintenance has been performed. Upon the transfer or sale of the aircraft, the owner is also required to transfer the appropriate records to a new owner. The owner or operator is also required to present maintenance records for inspection by the FAA or the National Transportation Safety Board (NTSB) when requested to do so.

RECORDS REQUIRED
The requirements for the appropriate maintenance records are contained in 14 CFR Part 91.417. This regulation requires that the owner or operator of an aircraft keep and maintain a record of the alterations, maintenance, 100-hour, annual, progressive and other inspections required on the airframe, each engine, propeller, rotor, and appliance. The owner must maintain a record of the aircraft's total time in service, current status of life-limited parts, time since overhaul on all items requiring overhaul, and the current status of applicable airworthiness directives. [Figure 7-1]

As part of these requirements, ADs should be chronologically listed and include the amendment number, revision date, the method of compliance, and if the AD is recurring, the time or date action is next required. Alterations to the aircraft must also be reflected in the permanent maintenance records along with an FAA Form 337 for each major alteration. Major repairs are recorded in the permanent maintenance records with a

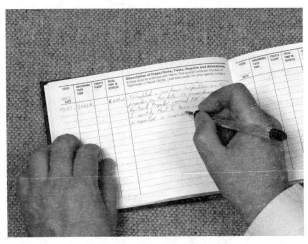

Figure 7-1. The requirement for maintaining appropriate records are contained in 14 CFR Part 91.417. It is important that a licensed technician make the proper logbook entries after any maintenance.

reference to work orders when the repairs have been done by a properly certified repair station, or by a Form 337 that provides details of the major repair and approving the aircraft for return to service.

Maintenance logbook formats vary significantly between aircraft manufacturers. Some logs are simply stapled paperback books, while others are hardbound and divided by index tabs to make locating pertinent sections more discernable. Remember that logbook condition is often construed as reflecting the care that the aircraft has received. To retain maximum value, it is important to keep maintenance records neat and organized, with an established chronology of maintenance history. For example, quality logbooks are tabbed or have another method for quickly referencing specific events such as inspections, alterations, repairs, etc. The owner has the option of changing logbook formats, and may want to consider investing in a logbook that provides a better organized method of tracking maintenance activities.

AIRFRAME RECORD
The airframe record for most small general aviation aircraft is combined into an Aircraft Logbook, which includes general information with regard to the entire aircraft. This logbook is used to record the time in service, maintenance, alterations, inspections and AD compliance on the airframe and its associated components and appliances. On large aircraft, turbine powered aircraft,

and helicopters, a separate Airframe Logbook may contain only a record of the maintenance of the airframe with separate logs for the appliances, component parts, and rotors.

ENGINE RECORDS

For most small general aviation aircraft, the engine log is maintained to record the time-in service, maintenance, alterations, inspection status, and AD compliance on the engine, propeller and its associated parts and appliances. Large and turbine-powered aircraft and helicopters often use separate logs for the propeller, appliances and parts of the engine that are changed frequently or that are life-limited components.

It is left up to the discretion of the owner whether maintenance activities on the propeller are recorded in the engine logbook, or in a separate propeller log. Most owners prefer to keep the propeller records in a separate document, since ownership of the propeller may be transferred without the engine. The separate log allows easy transfer of the propeller's time-in-service, maintenance actions, and AD status.

REBUILT ENGINE RECORDS

When an engine is originally manufactured, the time-in-service on the engine begins and normally continues until the engine is retired from service with one exception. This is when the engine is rebuilt by the manufacturer or an agency approved by the manufacturer. The old engine maintenance records can than be destroyed and the total time in service begins again from zero hours. This rule is contained in FAR Part 91.421 and It should be noted that the key word In the regulation is rebuilt. This rule does not apply to those engines that are remanufactured, reconditioned, or overhauled by aviation companies other than those approved by the manufacturer. [Figure 7-2]

Figure 7-2. When an engine is rebuilt by the manufacturer or its approved agency, its time-in service records begin with zero hours.

PROPELLER RECORDS

The propeller maintenance record is required to maintain the total time in service, maintenance, alterations, inspections and AD compliance on a propeller. On many light general aviation aircraft having a fixed-pitch propeller, this record is combined with the engine log as the propeller usually stays with the same engine throughout its service-life. It is often necessary however, to use a separate maintenance record to comply with the requirements of 14 CFR Part 91.417 in properly documenting the time in service and maintenance on a propeller, especially if the propeller has extensive overhaul requirements, applicable ADs, or other conditions that should be readily discerned. [Figure 7-3]

Figure 7-3. Propeller records are often kept in a separate logbook because a propeller may be exchanged many times between engines.

ROTOR RECORDS

A special record is required on the rotors of a helicopter or rotorcraft to maintain the time-in-service, maintenance, alterations, and AD compliance. The rotors on a helicopter are usually a life-limited part and the time in service of the rotors can be more readily determined if a separate record, other than the airframe log, is used to document the operating time. If the airframe log is used to document the maintenance and time-in-service, the log must contain sufficient information to clearly establish the life-limiting status of the rotors. [Figure 7-4]

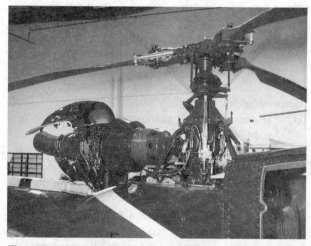

Figure 7-4. Helicopter rotors have special records to help determine the time-in-service status.

APPLIANCE RECORDS

Whenever an appliance is installed on an airframe or engine and it is considered a life-limited or a required time-overhaul component, it must have a record of its time in service, maintenance, alterations and AD compliance. A separate record of the appliance would be the most appropriate method of documenting this information. If the airframe or engine log is used to document this information, it must contain sufficient details to clearly establish the status of the time in service of these appliances.

MAINTENANCE RELEASE TAG

Certificated repair stations frequently use special parts condition tags to document the condition of parts and appliances. These tags are also used as a maintenance record and to track the time-in-service and overhaul times of components. These tags are often attached to the container or bag that the part is shipped in, and must remain with the component. When a part or appliance is repaired or overhauled, this tag is also considered the maintenance release or the return to service authorization for the individual appliance or part and should be retained in the logs for further reference until the component is permanently removed from the aircraft. [Figure 7-5]

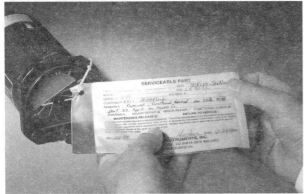

Figure 7-5. Airworthiness parts tags, used by certified repair stations, document condition of parts.

AIRWORTHINESS DIRECTIVE RECORD

The record of airworthiness directive compliance is sometimes incorporated into the body of maintenance record entries. A separate record can also be used for this purpose or a combination of recording ADs in the body of the maintenance record entries. A separate record makes it much easier to research and determine AD compliance during inspections. Some logbooks contain a section specifically designed to record the original compliance with AD notes and a separate area for retaining a cumulative list of ADs. This is especially beneficial since the cumulative lists must be amended and kept up-to-date during each airworthiness inspection. Logbooks are even available that provide a pouch for retaining the cumulative AD list as a loose document, or the lists may be retained in a separate binder.

When a separate binder is used, it should be clearly marked with the make, model, serial number, and registration number of the aircraft.

The appendix of this book has a suggested format that satisfies the requirements of 14 CFR Part 91.417 and provides the owner and maintenance personnel with an easy and reliable method of documenting and researching the AD compliance on an aircraft.

FORMAT OF MAINTENANCE RECORDS

There is no specified format or form for maintenance records. The records can be combined or separate in nature. Whatever is the most advantageous, and satisfies the requirements of 14 CFR Part 91.417 is acceptable. The important thing is to have a system that provides the necessary information in an organized format. It does not have to be a bound record such as found with most traditional logbooks. But, if separate unbound pages are used, it is desirable to number the pages in the book. [Figure 7-6]

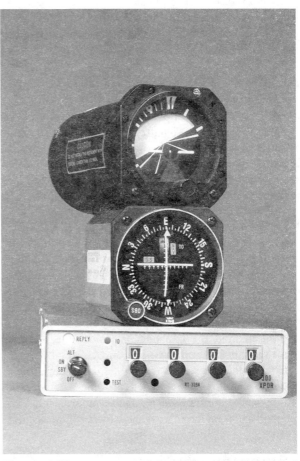

Figure 7-6. When a new or exchanged component is installed on an aircraft, an appropriate logbook entry is required to track the component's total time-in-service, and maintenance actions such as servicing, overhauls, and AD status

Separate records for each engine, propeller and appliance may be desirable when life-limited parts are

7-3

affected or if a large fleet operator desires to change components from one aircraft to another.

REQUIRED RECORD INFORMATION

The maintenance records should be identified as to the aircraft registration number, make, model, serial number, and where multiple engines or propellers are installed, the location of where each item is installed.

As previously mentioned, information to be included in the records consists of the total time in service of the items, the current status of life-limited parts, the time since last overhaul of items requiring overhaul on a time basis, current status of applicable airworthiness directives including the method of compliance, revision date, and if a recurring AD, the time or date when the next action is required, and a list of current major alterations to each air frame, engine, propeller, and appliance.

When maintenance is performed, the record entry must include the date that the work was completed, a description or reference to data acceptable to the FAA for the work performed, and the name, signature, and certificate type and number of the person approving the work for return to service.

RETENTION OF MAINTENANCE RECORDS

14 CFR Part 91.417 allows the owner to discard certain parts of the records after they have served their purpose. It also lists the records that must be retained. Records that must be retained are called permanent records and records that may be discarded are called temporary records.

PERMANENT RECORDS

Permanent records are those that contain the total time in service of the airframe, the current status of life-limited parts, the time since last overhaul of items to be overhauled on a time basis, the current status of the inspections required on the aircraft and its appliances, the current status of applicable airworthiness directives and the method of compliance, revision date, amendment number and if the AD is recurring, the time and date when the next action is required, and a current list of the major alterations to each airframe, engine, propeller, rotor, and appliance. These records must be retained and transferred to the new owner if the aircraft is sold.

TEMPORARY RECORDS

The maintenance record entries for maintenance and inspections, excluding those that fall into the category of permanent records, shall be retained until the work is repeated or superseded by other work, or for at least one year after the work is performed. This does not mean that these records must be discarded, but allows the owner to discard them if so desired.

LOST OR DESTROYED RECORDS

Whenever the maintenance records are lost or destroyed, the owner is responsible for reconstructing a new record. One acceptable method of starting a replacement record is for the owner or operator to make a notarized statement in the new record describing the loss of the original records and establishing the time in service of the aircraft or component. Establishing the time in service can be done by a research of other records that may contain that information.

The current status of the inspection on the aircraft, the status of life-limited parts, times since last overhaul, and a current list of major alterations will also have to be determined. One pretense that is used is that if the status of these items is unknown, they are considered to be unairworthy until their condition is determined. In most cases, the component or part must be disassembled or even overhauled to establish the condition of the part. This could prove to be very expensive for the owner of the aircraft. The status of applicable airworthiness directives must also be determined. This requires a detailed inspection, often requiring major disassembly of parts, to determine compliance with all applicable ADs.

RECORDING OF MAJOR REPAIRS AND ALTERATIONS

As previously discussed in chapter 5, whenever a major repair or major alteration is performed on an aircraft, the work is usally approved for return to service by the use of an FAA Form 337, (Major Repair and Alteration form). This form is initially completed by the technician performing the work and then submitted to an individual authorized by the FAA to approve the aircraft to service once the work has been completed.

A certificated repair station may substitute the maintenance release or work order in place of the Form 337 for major repairs but must use Form 337 for major alterations. Either information must be retained with the aircraft's permanent maintenance records.

STUDY QUESTIONS

1. Who is primarily responsible for the maintenance records of an aircraft?

2. Must an owner of an aircraft present the maintenance records to the FAA if they request them?

3. When can an engine that has been in service be returned to zero time in service?

4. Why is a separate record needed on a rotor of a helicopter?

5. When may it be necessary or more desirable to use a separate maintenance record for a propeller on an aircraft?

6. List the items that make up the permanent maintenance records on an aircraft?

7. What FAA form is used to approve a major alteration for return to service?

8. If the maintenance records are lost, who must initiate a new set of records?

9. How long must the information in the temporary maintenance records be retained?

Chapter 8
Maintenance Record Content and Entries

AIRCRAFT REPAIR ENTRIES

The minimum content of a maintenance record entry is listed in 14 CFR Part 43.9 and consists of the completion date of the work performed, a description or reference to data acceptable to the FAA, the name and if returned to service, the signature and certificate number of the person approving the aircraft, airframe, engine, propeller, or appliance for return to service.

A typical sample entry is given as follows:

Sample Entry

June 6, 1992

Replaced the alternator on the left engine with a new Prestolite model ALF-2017 S/N 10-12578, in accordance with chapter 12 of the Starcraft Service Manual.

Harold B. Nelson
AP No. 1643872

CERTIFICATED REPAIR STATION ENTRIES

Certificated repair stations are allowed to use an entry procedure that is different from maintenance personnel who return their work to service with the authorization of their technician's certificate.

The procedure used by a certificated repair station for a major repair is to give the customer a signed work order upon which the maintenance is recorded. A duplicate copy of the work order is retained, and a maintenance release statement is placed in the owner's maintenance record, indicating the number of the work order, and signed by an authorized representative of the repair station. A sample maintenance release statement follows:

Sample Entry

The aircraft, airframe, aircraft engine, propeller; or appliance identified above was repaired and inspected in accordance with current regulations of the FAA and is approved for return to service.

Pertinent details of the repair are on file at this repair station under order

No. 286   Date: June 6, 1992

Signed signature of authorized representative for

James Rogers

Repair Station Name *Rogers Aircraft Ser*
Certificate Number   *564 - 14*

AIRCRAFT INSPECTION ENTRIES

The maintenance record entries for the approval for return to service after inspections have been performed are specified in 14 CFR Part 43.11. This regulation requires an entry in the maintenance records containing the date of the inspection, total time in service. certification statement. type of inspection, signature, and certificate number of the person approving or disapproving for return to service of the aircraft, airframe, engine, propeller, or appliance.

ANNUAL INSPECTION ENTRY

An annual inspection can be signed off in the maintenance records as airworthy or unairworthy depending on the condition of the aircraft. A sample entry for the approval for the return to service after an annual inspection is as follows:

Sample Entry

June 6, 1992   Total Time: 550 Hours

I certify that this aircraft has been inspected in accordance with an annual inspection and was determined to be in airworthy condition.

George L. Smith
I.A. No. 1436721

UNAIRWORTHY INSPECTION PROCEDURE

When an inspector completes an inspection and finds that the aircraft is unairworthy, the inspector enters the completion of the inspection in the maintenance records indicating the aircraft's unairworthiness and a list of discrepancies are given to the owner of the aircraft. The owner is then required to have the discrepancies repaired before the aircraft can be flown.

These discrepancies are signed off by the appropriate person in the maintenance records as a repair entry, returning the aircraft to service. A sample entry indicating the completion of an annual Inspection as unairworthy is as follows:

Sample Entry

June 6, 1992   Total Time: 820 Hours

I certify that this aircraft has been inspected in accordance with an annual inspection and a list of discrepancies and unairworthy items dated June 6, 1985 has been provided for the aircraft owner.

Thomas Kingery
I.A. No. 1643782

A letter to the aircraft's owner, listing the discrepancies that made the aircraft unairworthy would be the best method of ensuring complete protection for the inspector and gives the proper notification to the owner.

Sample Letter

Jasper, Iowa

June 6, 1992

Mr. James Johnson
126 Norwood Drive
Jasper, Iowa

Dear Mr. Johnson:
This is to certify that on June 6, 1992, 1 completed an annual inspection on your aircraft Cessna 172L, Serial No. 17264837, N 2863A, located at the Northwoods Airports, and found it to be in unairworthy condition for the following reasons:

1. Left magneto has severely burned contact points.

2. Flame tubes in the muffler are broken loose.

Your aircraft will be considered to be in airworthy condition when the above listed discrepancies have been corrected and approved for return to service by a person authorized in 14 CFR Part 43.

John M. Smith
I.A. No. 1643782

100-HOUR INSPECTION ENTRY
A 100 hour inspection may be signed off in the maintenance records as airworthy or unairworthy depending on the condition of the aircraft. This is accomplished by using the same procedures as listed in the preceding paragraphs and substituting "100 hour" in place of the "annual" wording.

A sample entry for the completion of a 100-hour inspection is as follows:

Sample Entry

June 6, 1992   Total Time: 624 Hours

I certify that this aircraft. has been inspected in accordance with a 100-hour inspection and has been determined to be in airworthy condition.

John Lawson
A&P No. 1642375

PROGRESSIVE INSPECTION ENTRY
A sample entry for the approval for return to service after a progressive Inspection is as follows:

Sample Entry

June 6, 1992   Total Time: 624 Hours

I certify that in accordance with a progressive inspection program, a routine inspection of the left wing and a detailed inspection of the engine were performed in accordance with a progressive inspection and the aircraft is approved for return to service.

Harold B. Nelson
I.A. No. 1238645

APPROVED INSPECTION PROGRAM ENTRY
An approved inspection program entry will include the kind of inspection conducted and a statement that the inspection was performed in accordance with the instructions and procedures for the inspection program selected by the owner or operator of the airplane. If any defects or discrepancies discovered during the inspection are not repaired, a signed and dated list of those discrepancies will be given to the aircraft owner or operator.

An entry for an approved inspection would be as follows:

Sample Entry

June 21, 1992   Total Time: 1428 Hours

I certify that in accordance with an Approved Inspection Program, a 50 hour inspection was performed in accordance with the Starjet approved inspection manual and the aircraft is approved for return to service.

Roger L. Smith
A&P No. 1423876

AIRWORTHINESS DIRECTIVE COMPLIANCE ENTRIES

The information required in the maintenance records for the compliance of airworthiness directives is given in 14 CFR Part 91.173. The requirements consist of the recording of the date, total time, AD number, AD revision date, amendment number method of compliance and if the AD requires recurring action, the time and date when the next action is required. The name, signature, and certificate number of the individual performing the AD actions must be included for each original AD compliance.

The recording of AD compliance can be maintained in the body of a logbook entry and/or kept as a separate listing in the maintenance records.

ONE-TIME AD COMPLIANCE ENTRY

Sample Entry

June 30, 1992   Total Time: 826 hours

AD 76-03-05, revision date, Feb. 17, 1976, complied with by installing bracket in accordance with Paragraph B.

Thomas Kingery

A&P No. 1432652

RECURRING AD COMPLIANCE ENTRY

Sample Entry

June 26, 1992   Total Time: 1248 Hours

AD 76-05-04, revision date, July 12, 1976, complied with by inspecting the stabilizer attachment in accordance with paragraphs A and B. Next inspection is due at 2,248 hours.

John Lawson

A&P No. 1642375

AD COMPLIANCE LISTING FORMAT AND ENTRIES

A listing format may be used to show when the ADs were complied with and what method was used for the compliance. Some logbooks have provisions for these entries. See Appendix A for a sample listing format and how it is used.

FORM 337, MAJOR ALTERATION AND REPAIR

In completing the form, the person performing the repair fills out the form except for the approval for return to service block. This block will be filled out when the repair is inspected by an authorized person. The back of the form is used to describe the repair and the approved data that was followed to perform the repair. It should be noted that approved information and instructions were followed in making the repair and these instructions must be identified and listed. The inspector can only approve the repair for return to service if approved data and instructions were used to perform the repair and the work was performed in an airworthy manner.

DISPOSITION OF COMPLETED FORM 337

Two copies of Form 337 must be completed and signed. The original copy should be provided to the aircraft owner to be placed in the aircraft maintenance records, and one copy should be sent to the local FAA District Office within 48 hours of the approval for return to service of the aircraft, engine, propeller, or appliance that was repaired.

PREVENTIVE MAINTENANCE RECORDING REQUIREMENTS

The owner or operator of an aircraft is allowed to perform preventive maintenance functions, providing he or she holds at least a private pilot's certificate. Preventive maintenance is maintenance that is minor in nature that requires performing no complex disassembly or reassembly.

When preventive maintenance is performed, a maintenance record entry must be made with the following information:

- Date
- Description of work performed
- Name of the individual performing the work if other than the certifying individual.
- Certificate type and number
- Signature of the authorizing individual

The certificate type can be abbreviated using PP for private pilot, CP for commercial pilot, or ATP for Airline Transport Pilot certificates.

STUDY QUESTIONS

1. List the five items that are to be included in an approval for return to service after a repair was completed.

2. Who can approve the aircraft for return to service after maintenance has been performed in a certificated repair station?

3. List the minimum information required to approve an aircraft for return to service following a 100hour inspection.

4. True or false -when an annual inspection is completed and the aircraft is unairworthy, a list of unairworthy items must be given to the owner or operator.

5 Can a 100 hour inspection be signed off as unairworthy using the procedure thet is used to declare an annual inspection unairworthy?

6. List the minimum required information used to sign off a recurring airworthiness directive.

7. How many copies of the FAA Form 337 are required to approve a major repair to service?

8. Who gets the copies of the FAA Form 337?

Chapter 9
Pilot-In-Command Airworthiness Checks

The Pilot-in-Command (PIC) of an aircraft bears the responsibility of being the final and ultimate party that determines the airworthiness of their aircraft. This decision is made every time the pilot prepares to take a flight, even if it involves the same aircraft on the same day. The PIC has a very serious responsibility, and therefore many areas of airworthiness must be reviewed prior to making this decision. If a questionable situation arises, consulting a flight instructor or maintenance technician is extremely beneficial in making an airworthiness judgment.

Under 14 CFR part 91.7, no person may operate an aircraft unless it is in an airworthy condition, and the PIC of the aircraft determines that the aircraft is in condition for safe flight. Additionally, 14 CFR Part 91.405 outlines the maintenance responsibility of the owner/operator, whereas the PIC is considered to be an operator. Therefore, the PIC must ensure that the aircraft is inspected in accordance with 14 CFR part 91 subpart E, discrepancies are repaired in accordance with 14 CFR part 43, and appropriate entries are made in the maintenance records as outlined in 14 CFR part 91.417.

This chapter examines, in depth, the inspections and checks that must be confirmed by the PIC before a determination of airworthiness can be made. [Figure 9-1.]

A.R.O.W.
This acronym, often taught as a memory tool, is a list of the documents required to be onboard an aircraft while conducting flight operations. Most pilots use this as a part of their preflight checklist. The four letters stand for: Airworthiness Certificate, Registration, Operating Limitations, and Weight and Balance data. At one time there was an additional "R" included in the "ARROW" acronym which stood for a radio station license. Today, however, the FCC radio station license is no longer required unless the aircraft is operated across international borders.

AIRWORTHINESS CERTIFICATE
An airworthiness certificate is issued to every aircraft upon the completion of an inspection at the end of the manufacturing phase. This certificate signifies that the FAA has deemed that particular airplane as being in a condition of airworthiness. In accordance with FAA regulations, the certificate must be kept in the aircraft at all times and can typically be found in a plastic pouch mounted on the back of a seat or other part of the interior upholstery. [Figure 9-2] The certificate is issued without an expiration date. However, in order for the Airworthiness Certificate to remain valid, the aircraft must be maintained in an airworthy manner in accordance with the regulation under which the certificate was issued.

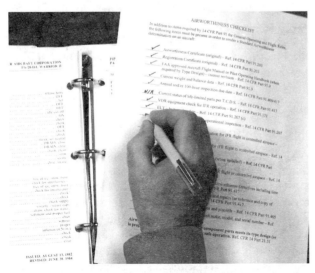

Figure 9-1. An airworthiness checklist, such as the one shown here, is beneficial for the PIC to use before any flight. It's especially useful before a pilot takes a check ride from an FAA Inspector or Designated Examiner.

Figure 9-2. The airworthiness certificate must be prominently displayed in the aircraft.

9-1

REGISTRATION

A US registration certificate, or the appropriate duplicate copy, is required to be inside the aircraft at all times. The registration must also be effective, in that the aircraft is registered in the United States to the correct individual or organization. The registration certificate is required by 14 CFR Part 91.203, but the actual rules governing the issuance of this certificate are included under 14 CFR Part 47.

OPERATING LIMITATIONS

For some older aircraft below 6,000 pounds gross weight, operating limitations can be conveyed to the pilot in the form of placards and instrument range markings. For newer aircraft, however, the operating limitations are typically outlined in chapter 2 of an Aircraft Flight Manual (AFM) or a Pilots Operating Handbook (POH). These limitations include weight limitations, maximum and minimum airspeeds, and other design features that limit the operational capabilities of the aircraft. For aircraft that require an FAA approved Flight Manual, the pilot must have the document onboard the aircraft and must also maintain a working knowledge of the operating limits.

Prior to 1979, only aircraft weighing more than 6,000 pounds gross weight were required to have an approved AFM. Due to the lack of consistent information available to pilots of smaller aircraft, the aviation industry, through the General Aviation Manufacturers Association (GAMA), introduced a new industry standard in 1975 for the publication of pilot operating handbooks. The FAA adopted this standard as a regulatory change in 1979. After this time, all new aircraft were required to have an FAA approved aircraft flight manual. As a result of this change, the source of information in the aircraft may be referred to as an AFM or a POH. The POH is required however to bear a statement that it is the FAA approved AFM. This statement is generally found within the first few pages of the publication. To determine if an FAA approved flight manual is required, the PIC should refer to the TCDS for the aircraft. [Figure 9-3]

For all aircraft, certain limitations must be displayed in the cockpit in the form of placards and markings, as prescribed in the TCDS. In addition, some placards are required to be displayed on the exterior of the aircraft to meet airworthiness certification standards. For example, most newer reciprocating engine-powered airplanes must have the word "Avgas" and the minimum grade fuel placarded near each fuel filler opening. If required placards or instrument markings become illegible or missing, the PIC should notify maintenance and discontinue operation of the aircraft until the discrepancy is corrected.

Figure 9-3. Whether its called an AFM or POH, it contains the same information in a standardized format.

WEIGHT AND BALANCE DATA

The weight and balance information is found in chapter 6 of the AFM or the POH, or for aircraft not required to have an approved manual, weight and balance information may be provided either as a separate document, or by a loading schedule placarded within the aircraft. Typically included in the approved manual is a listing of the original equipment installed in the aircraft as well as weight and balance data, records, and procedures. The total weight and center of gravity information must be kept up to date as items are added or removed from the aircraft. It is the responsibility of the pilot in command to determine the weight and balance of the aircraft prior to every flight to ensure the passenger, baggage and fuel loads are within the design limitations for the aircraft.

The equipment list maintained within the weight and balance information is vitally important to the pilot to determine if a piece of equipment is considered part of the aircraft empty weight. When the PIC determines the loading of an aircraft before flight, items such as tow bars, wheel chocks, fire extinguishers and others must be considered if they have not already been calculated into the empty weight data.

INSPECTION RECORDS

Airworthiness cannot be made by merely determining that the appropriate documents are onboard the aircraft. The inspection record of the aircraft must be investigated as well. Inspections that are not made within the time requirements outlined in the CFRs render the aircraft unairworthy. It is imperative to understand the inspections required for an aircraft and where that information is located. Typically, all maintenance records are located in the aircraft logbooks which are often divided into separate records for the airframe, engine, avionics, and propeller. For a check ride with the FAA, the pilot is required to produce evidence of inspections as well as possess a general understanding of the mandatory inspections.

There are several inspections that are required including:

- Annual or alternate airworthiness inspection program
- 100 hour
- AD compliance
- Emergency Locator Transmitter (ELT)
- Transponder/Mode C
- Altimeter/static system
- VOR Check

ANNUAL/100 HOUR INSPECTIONS

Annual inspections are mandatory every 12 calendar months for most smaller general aviation aircraft as stated in 14 CFR Part 91.409. Additionally, the aircraft must be approved for return to service by an IA after the inspection is complete. The inspection record and return to service entry are found in the maintenance log book. [Figure 9-4] A 100 hour inspection is required only for aircraft used in flight instruction for hire, or carrying persons for hire. This inspection must be completed every 100 hours, with a 10 hour extension provided only for the purposes of moving the aircraft to a location where the inspection can be conducted.

As an alternative to an annual inspection, the FAA provides other methods for inspecting an aircraft for airworthiness. As previously discussed in chapter 2, other programs include progressive, continuous, manufacturers', and FAA approved owner submitted inspection programs. When an alternative is used, the PIC must be aware of the type of inspection program and its status. For example, a progressive inspection requires a schedule that allows for the inspection of the aircraft in phases, with all phases being completed within 12 calendar months. Before flight, the PIC should confirm the inspection status by referring to the aircraft maintenance records, or have a reporting system in place that provides the PIC with the inspection status information.

The PIC should also understand what authorizations the inspection program provides for. For example,

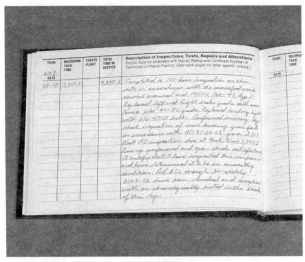

Figure 9-4. An annual inspection log book entry may look similar to the one shown here. Other inspection programs will have similarly worded maintenance record entries. The PIC must determine that the aircraft is inspected in accordance with an FAA approved program, and that appropriate maintenance record entries have been completed, showing the status of the inspection schedule.

when a progressive inspection is used, it negates the need for an annual or 100-hour inspection as long as the aircraft is in compliance with the approved inspection schedule. In a similar manner, an annual inspection negates the need for a 100-hour inspection, providing the annual was conducted within the previous 100 hours operating time. A 100-hour inspection, however, cannot be used in lieu of an annual inspection.

AIRWORTHINESS DIRECTIVE COMPLIANCE

Any applicable Airworthiness Directive (AD) must be in compliance before an aircraft can be operated. As previously discussed in Chapter 2, each directive includes a method of compliance and a time allocation for compliance. In some cases, a one time replacement or repair is sufficient for compliance. In other cases, the AD requires recurring compliance by checking a part every year at the annual inspection or at some other specified time or date. In the same vein, an AD may require immediate compliance rendering all affected aircraft unairworthy until the AD is complied with.

In any case, maintenance technicians have the responsibility of researching the directives to ensure the aircraft is in compliance as a routine part of an airworthiness inspection. A chronological list of all applicable ADs should be maintained in the aircraft records for the airframe, powerplant(s), propeller(s), and installed appliances. Although it is the owner's responsibility to ensure the aircraft is in compliance with applicable directives, it is also the ultimate responsibility of the PIC to determine that all ADs are complied with before operating the aircraft.

EMERGENCY LOCATOR TRANSMITTERS

Emergency Locator Transmitters (ELT) provide critical information to a search and rescue operation regarding the current position of a downed aircraft. In order for an ELT to work properly however, it must be in a fully operational condition. As a result, specific checks are required on the ELT system.

First, in accordance with 14 CFR 91.207, the ELT installation must be inspected every 12 months. This inspection includes an examination of the actual installation for battery corrosion, operation of the controls and crash sensors, and proper installation. Additionally, the ELT must be turned on to determine correct signal emission from the antenna. [Figure 9-5]

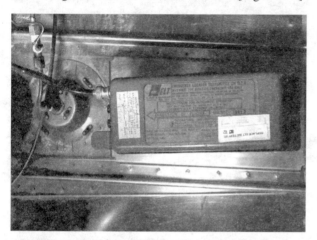

Figure 9-5. ELTs must be checked in accordance with regulations, and a maintenance record entry must be made showing the date the check was conducted.

Secondly, the battery itself must be checked as specified in 14 CFR 91.207. The date that the battery useful life expires must be marked clearly on the outside of the transmitter and an entry reflecting the expiration date made into the maintenance record. In addition, pilots need to be aware that the battery must be replaced when the ELT has been in use for 1 cumulative hour or more, or when 50% of the battery useful life has expired.

A provision for the removal of an ELT is outlined in 14 CFR 91.207. This allows for the removal of the ELT for maintenance and the operation of the aircraft without the ELT for a maximum of 90 days. When the ELT is initially removed, maintenance personnel must make a maintenance record entry reflecting the date, make, model and serial number of the ELT and reason for its removal. In addition, a placard must be installed in full view of the pilot that states "ELT not installed". After the permissible 90 days has lapsed, the aircraft is considered to be unairworthy if the ELT is not restored to the aircraft. There are also other allowances for aircraft to fly without an ELT, the most common being for training flights conducted within a 50 nautical mile radius of the departure airport only and scheduled air carrier operations.

TRANSPONDER TEST

A transponder must be inspected every 24 calendar months as required by 14 CFR Part 91.413. The inspection must be made in compliance with the criteria and method outlined in 14 CFR Part 43 Appendix F. Though seemingly insignificant, it is vitally important to entities such as Air Traffic Control (ATC) that a transponder is functioning properly and transmitting the correct information. ATC utilizes transponder information as a means of accurately and safely transitioning aircraft through the National Airspace System (NAS).

MODE C

While the altitude reporting system (Mode C) inspection is applicable only to aircraft flying in controlled airspace under instrument flight rules (IFR), failure to inspect this component renders an aircraft non-flyable in those operations due to unairworthiness. Every 24 calendar months, the automatic pressure altitude reporting system (Mode C) must be tested, inspected, and found to comply with 14 CFR Part 43 Appendix E. Further qualification for this inspection is included in 14 CFR Parts 91.217 and 91.411. An entry for the inspection of the above mentioned components should be made by the technician testing the system in the appropriate log book.

As mentioned, according to the regulations, the Mode C inspection and certification are required only for aircraft operating under IFR. It is important to note, however, that the Mode C is inspected as part of a transponder test, but it is not required to have an operational certification. The increasing dependence upon Traffic Alert and Collision Avoidance System (TCAS) also brings about serious issues regarding the inspection and certification of Mode C. TCAS is dependent upon accurate Mode C information emanating from aircraft in the vicinity. Though not specifically required on aircraft used only in VFR conditions, an inspection of the Mode C for accuracy should still be considered.

ALTIMETER/STATIC SYSTEM

Also before an aircraft can be operated in controlled airspace under IFR, in accordance with 14 CFR Part 91.411, each static pressure system and each altimeter instrument must be tested and inspected and found to comply with Part 43 Appendix E.

It is important to note that these inspections are not the same. One inspection requires the altimeter to be removed from the aircraft and checked against a certified standard at an FAA approved instrument repair station. In the test, the altimeter is placed in a vacuum chamber and checked for accuracy at 1,000-foot intervals up to the maximum certifiable altitude. The PIC should understand that if the altimeter is certified to an altitude that is lower than the maximum certified altitude for the aircraft, the aircraft operations become restricted to the lower altimeter certification altitude. For example, if an aircraft that is certified to operate at 30,000 feet has any altimeter installed that is only certified to 20,000 feet, the maximum altitude that the aircraft can be operated in controlled airspace under IFR is 20,000 feet.

In the other inspection, the static pressure system must be tested and inspected for leakage. In this test, the pressure is reduced in the aircraft's static system by a controlled vacuum source and then sealed off. After a prescribed period of time, the aircraft's altimeter reading is checked to determine if there is leakage in the system. Any leakage beyond specified limits requires repair. The inspection is normally conducted by an FAA certified instrument repair station, but there is an allowance for an airframe rated mechanic to do the test and inspection provided he or she has the proper equipment and experience to perform the work.

VOR CHECK

According to 14 CFR Part 91.171, in order to use an installed VOR system for navigation under IFR conditions, the VOR must be checked within 30 days of a proposed flight. Additionally, the VOR must meet the operational standards outlined in the aforementioned regulation. The VOR check can be made in a variety of ways including the use of a ground or airborne VOR checkpoint, VOR test facility (VOT), or dual VOR system check. VOR checks can be made by a pilot. If a check has not been made in the 30 days prior to the flight, a VOR check must be made prior to operating the aircraft under IFR.

Oftentimes, rental aircraft used for IFR training keep VOR check records in a prominently displayed location such as a clipboard or on the rental checkout sheet. For private aircraft however, this record is most likely only found in the aircraft maintenance records. While the VOR check does not specifically negate the airworthiness of the aircraft, IFR flight is severely limited without a VOR check being made within the proper time frame.

The PIC should keep in mind that maintenance personnel will not typically require this check to be made before returning an aircraft to service after an airworthiness inspection. Also, when a VOR check is conducted, an entry must be made in the appropriate record showing the date, location, bearing error, and signature of the individual making the check.

MAINTENANCE DISCREPANCIES/INOPERATIVE EQUIPMENT

Inspections and systems checks are extremely specific in that if the inspection is not made, the aircraft is unairworthy and not able to be flown. When the aircraft has maintenance discrepancies and inoperative equipment, however, it is not as straight forward a decision and requires a judgment call by the pilot in command.

Maintenance discrepancies, particularly with rental aircraft, are recorded in a notebook or on a clip board that is given to the renter. This is a venue by which a renter can notify the maintenance professionals and other pilots of problems encountered while flying the aircraft. It is the responsibility of the PIC to review the maintenance discrepancies that are open or deferred and determine if the aircraft is still airworthy and safe to fly.

An integral part of the airworthiness determination is understanding if and how inoperative equipment affects the aircraft. If an aircraft has a piece of inoperative equipment, there are three different methods by which to determine its airworthiness:

- Operations with a Minimum Equipment List (MEL) - 14 CFR part 91.213a, b, c

- Operations without a Minimum Equipment List or Master Minimum Equipment List (MMEL) - 14 CFR part 91.213d

- Operations with a Ferry Permit - 14 CFR part 91.213e

OPERATIONS WITH A MINIMUM EQUIPMENT LIST

A minimum equipment list (MEL) is a list of provisions for flight with inoperative equipment. This list is compiled by the operator based on the original master minimum equipment list (MMEL) developed by the FAA. An MEL is a document specific to an aircraft and must be accompanied by a letter of authorization (LOA) issued by the FAA giving permission for the MEL to be used. Together the MEL and the LOA constitute a supplemental type certificate (STC) thereby altering the original type certificate and providing authorization for flight in the altered condition.

Inoperative equipment requirements for aircraft with an MEL are outlined in 14 CFR Part 91.213. This regulation is very specific about the conditions that must be met before departing in an aircraft that has a piece of inoperative equipment. The PIC must be familiar with the use of the MEL, including the methods used to continue operating the aircraft with airworthiness deficiencies.[Figure 9-6]

Operations list in the POH or AFM, and any pertinent airworthiness directives. Equipment that is required by any of these documents renders the aircraft unairworthy and unable to be flown until repaired. [Figure 9-7]

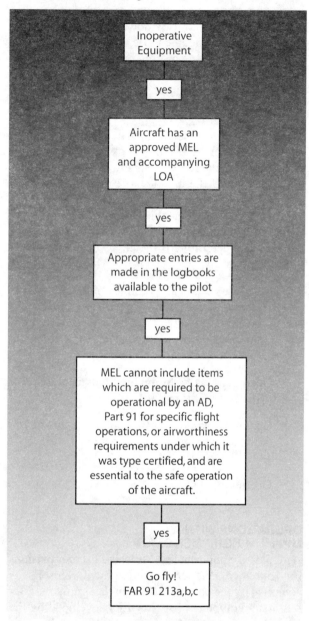

Figure 9-6. Determining continued airworthiness with inoperative equipment and an established MEL.

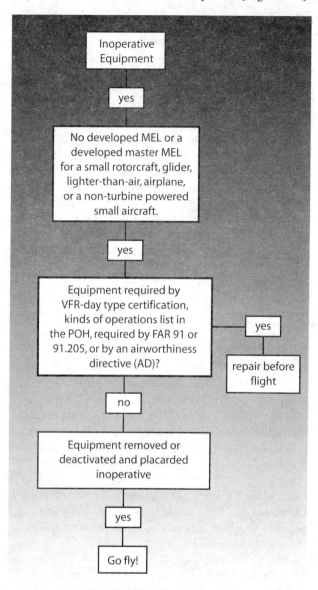

Figure 9-7. Determining continued airworthiness with inoperative equipment without an MEL.

OPERATIONS WITHOUT A MINIMUM EQUIPMENT LIST OR WITH A MASTER MINIMUM EQUIPMENT LIST

Also included in part 91 are guidelines for operating an aircraft with inoperative equipment without an established MEL and for a small rotorcraft, glider, lighter-than-air airplane, or a non-turbine powered small airplane with a developed Master MEL. Aircraft qualifying under these conditions must meet several documented references for required equipment including type certification, 14 CFR Part 91, Kind of

Anytime an aircraft is flown with inoperative equipment, the specific piece of equipment must be removed or deactivated. Additionally, as required by 14 CFR Part 43.11, the component must be placarded inoperative to prevent inadvertent use. An appropriate entry must be made in the maintenance logbook concerning the removal or deactivation of the inoperative component as well. [Figure 9-8]

OPERATIONS WITH A FERRY PERMIT

In accordance with 14 CFR Part 91.213e, an aircraft with inoperative equipment may be operated under the auspices of a special flight permit, also known as a ferry permit. The rules concerning the issuance of a ferry permit are outlined in 14 CFR Part 21.197 and

Figure 9-8. Inoperative equipment must be placarded.

21.199. This type of permit is typically issued for airplanes that need to be moved for maintenance, storage, customer delivery, or evacuation. Ferry permits are also granted for flight demonstrations and production flight testing. Flights conducted under a ferry permit, regardless of the reason for the flight, are made under strict limitations set forth by the FAA including:

- Flights over congested areas prohibited except for takeoff and landing
- Carriage of persons or cargo other than crew prohibited
- Daytime VFR flight only
- Crossing of international borders prohibited except where permission has been granted by the appropriate foreign government agency.

Ferry permits are obtained through an Airworthiness Inspector at a local FAA office. In order to issue the permit, the inspector must have information regarding the purpose of the flight, itinerary, required crew, restrictions necessary for safe operation, and a list of ways in which the aircraft does not meet airworthiness standards. Also, aircraft specific information must be submitted including the make, model and serial number. This information can be submitted in person as well as via phone/fax. While the owner is typically the one who requests a permit of this kind, a mechanic can request it provided the FAA receives a notification of permission to move the aircraft from the registered owner.

STUDY QUESTIONS

1. True or false. When an aircraft is sold, the airworthiness certificate should be returned to the FAA in Oklahoma City, Oklahoma.

2. How can a person determine if an Airplane Flight Manual is FAA-approved for a specific aircraft?

3. How can you determine if an AFM has all current revisions?

4. If an AD becomes due while on a flight, and the AD does not provide for an allowance for compliance, how may a person legally return to a location where the AD can be performed?

5. How long is a special airworthiness certificate (ferry permit) valid for?

APPENDIX A

AIRWORTHINESS CHECKLIST

In addition to items required by 14 CFR Part 91 for General Operating and Flight Rules, the following items must be present in order to render a Standard Airworthiness determination on an aircraft:

_____Airworthiness Certificate (original) – Ref. 14 CFR Part 91.203

_____Registration Certificate (original) – Ref. 14 CFR Part 91.203

_____FAA approved Aircraft Flight Manual or Pilot Operating Handbook (when required by Type Design) – current revision – Ref. 14 CFR Part 91.9

_____Current weight and balance data – Ref. 14 CFR Part 91.9

_____Annual and/or 100-hour inspection due date – Ref. 14 CFR Part 91.409/417

_____Current status of life-limited parts per T.C.D.S. – Ref. 14 CFR Part 91.417

_____VOR equipment check for IFR operation – Ref. 14 CFR Part 91.171

_____ELT – battery due date – Ref. 14 CFR Part 91.207 (c)

_____ELT – within last 12 months operational inspection – Ref. 14 CFR Part 91.207 (d)

_____Static System Inspection Certification for IFR flight in controlled airspace – Ref. 14 CFR Part 91.411

_____Altimeter Inspection Certification for IFR flight in controlled airspace – Ref. 14 CFR Part 91.413

_____Transponder Inspection Certification (when installed) – Ref. 14 CFR Part 91.413

_____Encoding Altimeter Certification for IFR flight in controlled airspace – Ref. 14 CFR Part 91.411

_____Current status listing of all applicable Airworthiness Directives including time or date of recurring action – Ref. 14 CFR Part 91.417

_____FAA Form 337s for major alterations and repairs (or reference and copy of work order for major repairs) – Ref. 14 CFR Part 91.417

_____Inoperative Equipment record entries and placards – Ref. 14 CFR Part 91.405

_____External Data Plate reflecting aircraft make, model, and serial number – Ref. 14 CFR Part 45.11

Airworthy means an aircraft or one of its component parts meets its type design (or is properly altered) and is in condition for safe operation. Ref. CFR 14 Part 21.31

APPENDIX B

14 CFR PART 43 MAINTENANCE, PREVENTIVE MAINTENANCE, REBUILDING, AND ALTERATION

MAINTENANCE RECORD ENTRIES—EXCERPT

§ 43.9 Content, form, and disposition of maintenance, preventive maintenance, rebuilding, and alteration records (except inspections performed in accordance with part 91, part 123, part 125, § 135.411(a)(1), and § 135.419 of this chapter).

(a) Maintenance record entries. Except as provided in paragraphs (b) and (c) of this section, each person who maintains, performs preventive maintenance, rebuilds, or alters an aircraft, airframe, aircraft engine, propeller, appliance, or component part shall make an entry in the maintenance record of that equipment containing the following information:

(1) A description (or reference to data acceptable to the Administrator) of work performed.

(2) The date of completion of the work performed.

(3) The name of the person performing the work if other than the person specified in paragraph (a)(4) of this section.

(4) If the work performed on the aircraft, airframe, aircraft engine, propeller, appliance, or component part has been performed satisfactorily, the signature, certificate number, and kind of certificate held by the person approving the work. The signature constitutes the approval for return to service only for the work performed. In addition to the entry required by this paragraph, major repairs and major alterations shall be entered on a form, and the form disposed of, in the manner prescribed in appendix B, by the person performing the work.

(b) Each holder of an air carrier operating certificate or an operating certificate issued under Part 121 or 135, that is required by its approved operations specifications to provide for a continuous airworthiness maintenance program, shall make a record of the maintenance, preventive maintenance, rebuilding, and alteration, on aircraft, airframes, aircraft engines, propellers, appliances, or component parts which it operates in accordance with the applicable provisions of Part 121 or 135 of this chapter, as appropriate.

(c) This section does not apply to persons performing inspections in accordance with Part 91, 123, 125, § 135.411(a)(1), or § 135.419 of this chapter.

[Amdt. 43-23, 47 FR 41085, Sept. 16, 1982, as amended by Amdt. 43-37, 66 FR 21066, Apr. 27, 2001]

§ 43.11 Content, form, and disposition of records for inspections conducted under parts 91 and 125 and §§ 135.411(a)(1) and 135.419 of this chapter.

(a) Maintenance record entries. The person approving or disapproving for return to service an aircraft, airframe, aircraft engine, propeller, appliance, or component part after any inspection performed in accordance with Part 91, 123, 125, § 135.411(a)(1), or § 135.419 shall make an entry in the maintenance record of that equipment containing the following information:

(1) The type of inspection and a brief description of the extent of the inspection.

(2) The date of the inspection and aircraft total time in service.

(3) The signature, the certificate number, and kind of certificate held by the person approving or disapproving for return to service the aircraft, airframe, aircraft engine, propeller, appliance, component part, or portions thereof.

(4) Except for progressive inspections, if the aircraft is found to be airworthy and approved for return to service, the following or a similarly worded statement — "I certify that this aircraft has been inspected in accordance with (insert type) inspection and was determined to be in airworthy condition."

(5) Except for progressive inspections, if the aircraft is not approved for return to service because of needed maintenance, noncompliance with applicable specifications, airworthiness directives, or other approved data, the following or a similarly worded statement — "I certify that this aircraft has been inspected in accordance with (insert type) inspection and a list of discrepancies and unairworthy items dated (date) has been provided for the aircraft owner or operator."

(6) For progressive inspections, the following or a similarly worded statement — "I certify that in accordance with a progressive inspection program, a routine inspection of (identify whether aircraft or components) and a detailed inspection of (identify components) were performed and the (aircraft or components) are (approved or disapproved) for return to service." If disapproved, the entry will further state "and a list of discrepancies and unairworthy items dated (date) has been provided to the aircraft owner or operator."

(7) If an inspection is conducted under an inspection program provided for in part 91, 123, 125, or § 135.411(a)(1), the entry must identify the inspection program, that part of the inspection program accomplished, and contain a statement that the inspection was performed in accordance with the inspections and procedures for that particular program.

(b) Listing of discrepancies and placards. If the person performing any inspection required by part 91 or 125 or § 135.411(a)(1) of this chapter finds that the aircraft is unairworthy or does not meet the applicable type certificate data, airworthiness directives, or other approved data upon which its airworthiness depends, that persons must give the owner or lessee a signed and dated list of those discrepancies. For those items permitted to be inoperative under § 91.213(d)(2) of this chapter, that person shall place a placard, that meets the aircraft's airworthiness certification regulations, on each inoperative instrument and the cockpit control of each item of inoperative equipment, marking it "Inoperative," and shall add the items to the signed and dated list of discrepancies given to the owner or lessee.

[Amdt. 43-23, 47 FR 41085, Sept. 16, 1982, as amended by Amdt. 43-30, 53 FR 50195, Dec. 13, 1988; Amdt. 43-36, 61 FR 19501, May 1, 1996]

§ 43.12 Maintenance records: Falsification, reproduction, or alteration.

(a) No person may make or cause to be made:

(1) Any fraudulent or intentionally false entry in any record or report that is required to be made, kept, or used to show compliance with any requirement under this part;

(2) Any reproduction, for fraudulent purpose, of any record or report under this part; or

(3) Any alteration, for fraudulent purpose, of any record or report under this part.

(b) The commission by any person of an act prohibited under paragraph (a) of this section is a basis for suspending or revoking the applicable airman, operator, or production certificate,

Technical Standard Order Authorization, FAA-Parts Manufacturer Approval, or Product and Process Specification issued by the Administrator and held by that person.

[Amdt. 43-19, 43 FR 22639, May 25, 1978, as amended by Amdt. 43-23, 47 FR 41085, Sept. 16, 1982]

APPENDIX C

14 CFR Part 43, Appendix D — INSPECTION ITEMS
Scope and Detail of Items (as Applicable to the Particular Aircraft) To Be Included in Annual and 100-Hour Inspections

(a) Each person performing an annual or 100-hour inspection shall, before that inspection, remove or open all necessary inspection plates, access doors, fairing, and cowling. He shall thoroughly clean the aircraft and aircraft engine.

(b) Each person performing an annual or 100-hour inspection shall inspect (where applicable) the following components of the fuselage and hull group:

(1) Fabric and skin — for deterioration, distortion, other evidence of failure, and defective or insecure attachment of fittings.

(2) Systems and components — for improper installation, apparent defects, and unsatisfactory operation.

(3) Envelope, gas bags, ballast tanks, and related parts — for poor condition.

(c) Each person performing an annual or 100-hour inspection shall inspect (where applicable) the following components of the cabin and cockpit group:

(1) Generally — for uncleanliness and loose equipment that might foul the controls.

(2) Seats and safety belts — for poor condition and apparent defects.

(3) Windows and windshields — for deterioration and breakage.

(4) Instruments — for poor condition, mounting, marking, and (where practicable) improper operation.

(5) Flight and engine controls — for improper installation and improper operation.

(6) Batteries — for improper installation and improper charge.

(7) All systems — for improper installation, poor general condition, apparent and obvious defects, and insecurity of attachment.

(d) Each person performing an annual or 100-hour inspection shall inspect (where applicable) components of the engine and nacelle group as follows:

(1) Engine section — for visual evidence of excessive oil, fuel, or hydraulic leaks, and sources of such leaks.

(2) Studs and nuts — for improper torquing and obvious defects.

(3) Internal engine — for cylinder compression and for metal particles or foreign matter on screens and sump drain plugs. If there is weak cylinder compression, for improper internal condition and improper internal tolerances.

(4) Engine mount — for cracks, looseness of mounting, and looseness of engine to mount.

(5) Flexible vibration dampeners — for poor condition and deterioration.

(6) Engine controls — for defects, improper travel, and improper safetying.

(7) Lines, hoses, and clamps — for leaks, improper condition and looseness.

(8) Exhaust stacks — for cracks, defects, and improper attachment.

(9) Accessories — for apparent defects in security of mounting.

(10) All systems — for improper installation, poor general condition, defects, and insecure attachment.

(11) Cowling — for cracks, and defects.

(e) Each person performing an annual or 100-hour inspection shall inspect (where applicable) the following components of the landing gear group:

(1) All units — for poor condition and insecurity of attachment.

(2) Shock absorbing devices — for improper oleo fluid level.

(3) Linkages, trusses, and members — for undue or excessive wear fatigue, and distortion.

(4) Retracting and locking mechanism — for improper operation.

(5) Hydraulic lines — for leakage.

(6) Electrical system — for chafing and improper operation of switches.

(7) Wheels — for cracks, defects, and condition of bearings.

(8) Tires — for wear and cuts.

(9) Brakes — for improper adjustment.

(10) Floats and skis — for insecure attachment and obvious or apparent defects.

(f) Each person performing an annual or 100-hour inspection shall inspect (where applicable) all components of the wing and center section assembly for poor general condition, fabric or skin deterioration, distortion, evidence of failure, and insecurity of attachment.

(g) Each person performing an annual or 100-hour inspection shall inspect (where applicable) all components and systems that make up the complete empennage assembly for poor general condition, fabric or skin deterioration, distortion, evidence of failure, insecure attachment, improper component installation, and improper component operation.

(h) Each person performing an annual or 100-hour inspection shall inspect (where applicable) the following components of the propeller group:

(1) Propeller assembly — for cracks, nicks, binds, and oil leakage.

(2) Bolts — for improper torquing and lack of safetying.

(3) Anti-icing devices — for improper operations and obvious defects.

(4) Control mechanisms — for improper operation, insecure mounting, and restricted travel.

(i) Each person performing an annual or 100-hour inspection shall inspect (where applicable) the following components of the radio group:

(1) Radio and electronic equipment — for improper installation and insecure mounting.

(2) Wiring and conduits — for improper routing, insecure mounting, and obvious defects.

(3) Bonding and shielding — for improper installation and poor condition.

(4) Antenna including trailing antenna — for poor condition, insecure mounting, and improper operation.

(j) Each person performing an annual or 100-hour inspection shall inspect (where applicable) each installed miscellaneous item that is not otherwise covered by this listing for improper installation and improper operation.

APPENDIX D

14 CFR PART 91.409 — INSPECTIONS

§ 91.409 Inspections.

(a) Except as provided in paragraph (c) of this section, no person may operate an aircraft unless, within the preceding 12 calendar months, it has had —

(1) An annual inspection in accordance with part 43 of this chapter and has been approved for return to service by a person authorized by § 43.7 of this chapter; or

(2) An inspection for the issuance of an airworthiness certificate in accordance with part 21 of this chapter. No inspection performed under paragraph (b) of this section may be substituted for any inspection required by this paragraph unless it is performed by a person authorized to perform annual inspections and is entered as an "annual" inspection in the required maintenance records.

(b) Except as provided in paragraph (c) of this section, no person may operate an aircraft carrying any person (other than a crewmember) for hire, and no person may give flight instruction for hire in an aircraft which that person provides, unless within the preceding 100 hours of time in service the aircraft has received an annual or 100-hour inspection and been approved for return to service in accordance with part 43 of this chapter or has received an inspection for the issuance of an airworthiness certificate in accordance with part 21 of this chapter. The 100-hour limitation may be exceeded by not more than 10 hours while en route to reach a place where the inspection can be done. The excess time used to reach a place where the inspection can be done must be included in computing the next 100 hours of time in service.

(c) Paragraphs (a) and (b) of this section do not apply to —

(1) An aircraft that carries a special flight permit, a current experimental certificate, or a provisional airworthiness certificate;

(2) An aircraft inspected in accordance with an approved aircraft inspection program under part 125 or 135 of this chapter and so identified by the registration number in the operations specifications of the certificate holder having the approved inspection program;

(3) An aircraft subject to the requirements of paragraph (d) or (e) of this section; or

(4) Turbine-powered rotorcraft when the operator elects to inspect that rotorcraft in accordance with paragraph (e) of this section.

(d) Progressive inspection. Each registered owner or operator of an aircraft desiring to use a progressive inspection program must submit a written request to the FAA Flight Standards district office having jurisdiction over the area in which the applicant is located, and shall provide —

(1) A certificated mechanic holding an inspection authorization, a certificated airframe repair station, or the manufacturer of the aircraft to supervise or conduct the progressive inspection;

(2) A current inspection procedures manual available and readily understandable to pilot and maintenance personnel containing, in detail —

(i) An explanation of the progressive inspection, including the continuity of inspection responsibility, the making of reports, and the keeping of records and technical reference material;

(ii) An inspection schedule, specifying the intervals in hours or days when routine and detailed inspections will be performed and including instructions for exceeding an inspection interval by not more than 10 hours while en route and for changing an inspection interval because of service experience;

(iii) Sample routine and detailed inspection forms and instructions for their use; and

(iv) Sample reports and records and instructions for their use;

(3) Enough housing and equipment for necessary disassembly and proper inspection of the aircraft; and

(4) Appropriate current technical information for the aircraft. The frequency and detail of the progressive inspection shall provide for the complete inspection of the aircraft within each 12 calendar months and be consistent with the manufacturer's recommendations, field service experience, and the kind of operation in which the aircraft is engaged. The progressive inspection schedule must ensure that the aircraft, at all times, will be airworthy and will conform to all applicable FAA aircraft specifications, type certificate data

sheets, airworthiness directives, and other approved data. If the progressive inspection is discontinued, the owner or operator shall immediately notify the local FAA Flight Standards district office, in writing, of the discontinuance. After the discontinuance, the first annual inspection under § 91.409(a)(1) is due within 12 calendar months after the last complete inspection of the aircraft under the progressive inspection. The 100-hour inspection under § 91.409(b) is due within 100 hours after that complete inspection. A complete inspection of the aircraft, for the purpose of determining when the annual and 100-hour inspections are due, requires a detailed inspection of the aircraft and all its components in accordance with the progressive inspection. A routine inspection of the aircraft and a detailed inspection of several components is not considered to be a complete inspection.

(e) Large airplanes (to which part 125 is not applicable), turbojet multiengine airplanes, turbopropeller-powered multiengine airplanes, and turbine-powered rotorcraft. No person may operate a large airplane, turbojet multiengine airplane, turbopropeller-powered multiengine airplane, or turbine-powered rotorcraft unless the replacement times for life-limited parts specified in the aircraft specifications, type data sheets, or other documents approved by the Administrator are complied with and the airplane or turbine-powered rotorcraft, including the airframe, engines, propellers, rotors, appliances, survival equipment, and emergency equipment, is inspected in accordance with an inspection program selected under the provisions of paragraph (f) of this section, except that, the owner or operator of a turbine-powered rotorcraft may elect to use the inspection provisions of § 91.409(a), (b), (c), or (d) in lieu of an inspection option of § 91.409(f).

(f) Selection of inspection program under paragraph (e) of this section. The registered owner or operator of each airplane or turbine-powered rotorcraft described in paragraph (e) of this section must select, identify in the aircraft maintenance records, and use one of the following programs for the inspection of the aircraft:

(1) A continuous airworthiness inspection program that is part of a continuous airworthiness maintenance program currently in use by a person holding an air carrier operating certificate or an operating certificate issued under part 121 or 135 of this chapter and operating that make and model aircraft under part 121 of this chapter or operating that make and model under part 135 of this chapter and maintaining it under § 135.411(a)(2) of this chapter.

(2) An approved aircraft inspection program approved under § 135.419 of this chapter and currently in use by a person holding an operating certificate issued under part 135 of this chapter.

(3) A current inspection program recommended by the manufacturer.

(4) Any other inspection program established by the registered owner or operator of that airplane or turbine-powered rotorcraft and approved by the Administrator under paragraph (g) of this section. However, the Administrator may require revision of this inspection program in accordance with the provisions of § 91.415. Each operator shall include in the selected program the name and address of the person responsible for scheduling the inspections required by the program and make a copy of that program available to the person performing inspections on the aircraft and, upon request, to the Administrator.

(g) Inspection program approved under paragraph (e) of this section. Each operator of an airplane or turbine-powered rotorcraft desiring to establish or change an approved inspection program under paragraph (f)(4) of this section must submit the program for approval to the local FAA Flight Standards district office having jurisdiction over the area in which the aircraft is based. The program must be in writing and include at least the following information:

(1) Instructions and procedures for the conduct of inspections for the particular make and model airplane or turbine-powered rotorcraft, including necessary tests and checks. The instructions and procedures must set forth in detail the parts and areas of the airframe, engines, propellers, rotors, and appliances, including survival and emergency equipment required to be inspected.

(2) A schedule for performing the inspections that must be performed under the program expressed in terms of the time in service, calendar time, number of system operations, or any combination of these.

(h) Changes from one inspection program to another. When an operator changes from one inspection program under paragraph (f) of this section to another, the time in service, calendar times, or cycles of operation accumulated under the previous program must be applied in determining inspection due times under the new program. (Approved by the Office of Management and Budget under control number 2120-0005) [Doc. No. 18334, 54 FR 34311, Aug. 18, 1989; Amdt. 91-211, 54 FR 41211, Oct. 5, 1989; Amdt. 91-267, 66 FR 21066, Apr. 27, 2001]

APPENDIX E

U.S. Department of Transportation
Federal Aviation Administration

Advisory Circular

Subject: **MAINTENANCE RECORDS**	Date: 6/8/98 Initiated by: AFS-340	AC No: 43-9C Change:

1. PURPOSE. This advisory circular (AC) describes methods, procedures and practices that have been determined to be acceptable means of showing compliance with the general aviation maintenance record making and record keeping requirements of Title 14 of the Code of Federal Regulations (14 CFR) parts 43 and 91. This material is not mandatory, nor is it regulatory and acknowledges that the Federal Aviation Administration (FAA) will consider other methods that may be presented. It is issued for guidance purposes and outlines several methods of compliance with the regulations.

> NOTE: The information in this AC does not apply to air carrier maintenance records made and retained in accordance with 14 CFR part 121.

2. CANCELLATION. AC 43-9B, Maintenance Records, dated January 9, 1984, is canceled.

3. RELATED REGULATIONS. 14 CFR parts 1, 43, 91, and 145.

4. DISCUSSION. The Code of Federal Regulations state that a U.S. standard airworthiness certificate is effective until it is surrendered, suspended, revoked, or a termination date is otherwise established by the Administrator. In addition to those terms, a U.S. standard airworthiness certificate is effective only as long as the maintenance, preventive maintenance, and alterations are performed in accordance with parts 43 and 91, and the aircraft are registered in the United States. These terms and conditions are further restated, in block 6, on the front of FAA Form 8100-2, Standard Airworthiness Certificate. Qualified persons, who perform the maintenance, preventive maintenance and alterations, shall make a record entry of this accomplishment, thus maintaining the validity of the certificate of airworthiness. Adequate aircraft records provide tangible evidence that the aircraft complies with the appropriate airworthiness requirements. In accordance with the terms and conditions listed in block 6 of the Standard Airworthiness Certificate, insufficient or non-existent aircraft records may render that standard airworthiness certificate invalid.

5. MAINTENANCE RECORD REQUIREMENTS.

a. Responsibilities. 14 CFR part 91, section 91.417 states that an aircraft owner/operator shall keep and maintain aircraft maintenance records. 14 CFR part 43, sections 43.9 and 43.11 state that maintenance personnel, however, are required to make the record entries.

b. Maintenance Records That Are to Be Retained. Section 91.405 requires each owner or operator to ensure that maintenance personnel make appropriate entries in the maintenance records to indicate that the aircraft has been approved for return to service. Section 91.417(a) sets forth the content requirements and retention requirements for maintenance records. Maintenance records may be kept in any format that provides record continuity; includes required contents; lends itself to the addition of new entries; provides for signature entry; and, is intelligible. Section 91.417(b) requires records of maintenance, alterations, and required or approved inspections to be retained until the work is repeated, superseded by other work, or for one year. It also requires the records, specified in section 91.417(a)(2), to be retained and transferred with the aircraft at the time of sale.

> **NOTE:** Section 91.417(a) contains an exception regarding work accomplished in accordance with section 91.411. This <u>does not</u> exclude the making of entries for this work, but applies to the retention period of the records for work done in accordance with this section. The exclusion is necessary since the retention period of one year is inconsistent with the 24-month interval of test and inspection specified in section 91.411. Entries for work done per this section are to be retained for 24 months or until the work is repeated or superseded.

c. Section 91.417(a)(1). Requires a record of maintenance, for each aircraft (including the airframe) and each engine, propeller, rotor, and appliance of an aircraft. This <u>does not</u> require separate or individual records for each of these items. It <u>does</u> require the information specified in sections 91.417(a)(1) through 91.417(a)(2)(vi) to be kept for each item as appropriate. As a practical matter, many owners and operators find it advantageous to keep separate or individual records since it facilitates transfer of the record with the item when ownership changes. Section 91.417(a)(1) has no counterpart in section 43.9 or section 43.11.

d. Section 91.417(a)(1)(i). Requires the maintenance record entry to include "a description of the work performed." The description should be in sufficient detail to permit a person unfamiliar with the work to understand what was done, and the methods and procedures used in doing it. When the work is extensive, this results in a voluminous record. To provide for this contingency, the rule permits reference to technical data acceptable to the Administrator in lieu of making the detailed entry. Manufacturer's manuals, service letters, bulletins, work orders, FAA AC's, and others, which accurately describe what was done, or how it was done, may be referenced. Except for the documents mentioned, which are in common usage, referenced documents are to be made a part of the maintenance records and retained in accordance with section 91.417(b).

> **NOTE: Certificated repair stations frequently work on components shipped to them without the maintenance records. To provide for this situation, repair stations should supply owners and operators with copies of work orders written for the work, in lieu of maintenance record entries. The work order copy must include the information, required by section 91.417(a)(1) through section 91.417(a)(1)(iii), be made a part of the maintenance record, and retained per section 91.417(b). This procedure is not the same as that for maintenance releases discussed in paragraph 16, and it may not be used when maintenance records are available. Section 91.417(a)(1)(i) is identical to its counterpart, section 43.9(a)(1), which imposes the same requirements on maintenance personnel.**

e. Section 91.417(a)(1)(ii). Is identical to section 43.9(a)(2) and requires entries to contain the date the work was completed. This is normally the date upon which the work is approved for return to service. However, when work is accomplished by one person and approved for return to service by another, the dates may differ. Two signatures may also appear under this circumstance; however, a single entry in accordance with section 43.9(a)(3) is acceptable.

f. Section 91.417(a)(1)(iii). Differs slightly from section 43.9(a)(4) in that it requires the entry to indicate only the signature and certificate number of the person approving the work for return to service, and does not require the type of certificate being exercised to be indicated as does section 43.9(a)(4). This is a new requirement of section 43.9(a)(4), which assists owners and operators in meeting their responsibilities. Maintenance personnel may indicate the type of certificate exercised by using airframe (A), powerplant (P), airframe & powerplant (A&P), inspection authorization (IA), or certificated repair station (CRS).

g. Section 91.417(a)(2). Requires six items to be made a part of the maintenance record and maintained as such. Section 43.9 does not require maintenance personnel to enter these items. Section 43.11 requires some of them to be part of entries made for inspections, but they are all the responsibility of the owner or operator. The six items are discussed as follows:

(1) Section 91.417(a)(2)(i). Requires a record of total time-in-service to be kept for the airframe, each engine, and each propeller. Part 1, section 1.1, Definitions, defines time in service, with respect to maintenance time records, as that time from the moment an aircraft leaves the surface of the earth until it touches down at the next point of landing. Section 43.9 does not require this to be part of the entries for maintenance, preventive maintenance, rebuilding, or alterations. However, section 43.11 requires maintenance personnel to make it a part of the entries for inspections made under parts 91, 125, and time-in-service in all entries.

(a) Some circumstances impact the owner's or operator's ability to comply with section 91.417(a)(2)(i). For example, in the case of rebuilt engines, the owner or operator would not have a way of knowing the total time-in-service, since section 91.421 permits the maintenance record to be discontinued and the engine time to be started at <u>zero</u>. In this case, the maintenance record and time-in-service, subsequent to the rebuild, comprise a satisfactory record.

(b) Many components, presently in-service, were put into service before the requirements to keep maintenance records on them. Propellers are probably foremost in this group. In these instances, practicable procedures for compliance with the record requirements must be used. For example, total time-in-service may be derived using the procedures described in paragraph 12; or if records prior to the regulatory requirements are just not available from any source, time-in-service may be kept since last complete overhaul. Neither of these procedures is acceptable when life-limited parts status is involved or when airworthiness directive (AD) compliance is a factor. Only the actual record since new may be used in these instances.

(c) Sometimes engines are assembled from modules (turbojet and some turbopropeller engines) and a true total time-in-service for the total engine is not kept. If owners and operators wish to take advantage of this modular design, then total time-in-service and a maintenance record for each module is to be maintained. The maintenance records specified in section 91.417(a)(2) are to be kept with the module.

(2) **Section 91.417(a)(2)(ii).** Requires the current status of life-limited parts to be part of the maintenance record. If total time-in-service of the aircraft, engine, propeller, etc., is entered in the record when a life-limited part is installed and the time-in-service of the life-limited part is included, the normal record of time-in-service automatically meets this requirement.

(3) **Section 91.417(a)(2)(iii).** Requires the maintenance record to indicate the time since last overhaul of all items installed on the aircraft that are required to be overhauled on a specified time basis. The explanation in paragraph 5g (2) also applies to this requirement.

(4) **Section 91.417(a)(2)(iv).** Deals with the current inspection status and requires it to be reflected in the maintenance record. Again, the explanation in paragraph 5g (2) is appropriate even though section 43.11(a)(2) requires maintenance persons to determine time-in-service of the item being inspected and to include it as part of the inspection entry.

(5) **Section 91.417(a)(2)(v).** Requires the current status of applicable AD's to be a part of the maintenance record. The record is to include, at minimum, the method used to comply with the AD, the AD number, and revision date; and if the AD has requirements for recurring

action, the time-in-service and the date when that action is required. When AD's are accomplished, maintenance persons are required to include the items specified in section 43.9(a)(2), (3), and (4) in addition to those required by section 91.417(a)(2)(v). An example of a maintenance record format for AD compliance is contained in Appendix 1.

(6) **Section 91.417(a)(2)(vi).** In the past, the owner or operator has been permitted to maintain a list of current major alterations to the airframe, engine(s), propeller(s), rotor(s), or appliances. This procedure did not produce a record of value to the owner/operator or to maintenance persons in determining the continued airworthiness of the alteration since such a record was not sufficient detail. This section of the rule has now been changed. It now prescribes that copies of FAA Form 337, issued for the alteration, be made a part of the maintenance record.

6. PREVENTIVE MAINTENANCE.

a. Preventive maintenance is defined in part 1, section 1.1. Part 43, appendix A, paragraph (c) lists those items which a pilot may accomplish under section 43.3(g). Section 43.7 authorizes appropriately rated repair stations and mechanics, and persons holding at least a private pilot certificate to approve an aircraft for return to service after they have performed preventive maintenance. All of these persons must record preventive maintenance accomplished in accordance with the requirements of section 43.9. AC 43-12, Preventive Maintenance, current edition, contains further information on this subject.

b. The type of certificate exercised when maintenance or preventive maintenance is accomplished must be indicated in the maintenance record. Pilots may use private pilot (PP), commercial pilot (CP), or air transport pilot (ATP) to indicate private, commercial, or airline transport pilot certificate, respectively, in approving preventive maintenance for return to service. Pilots are not authorized by section 43.3(g) to perform preventive maintenance on aircraft when they are operated under part 121, 127, 129, or 135. Pilots may only approve for return to service preventive maintenance that they themselves have accomplished.

7. REBUILT ENGINE MAINTENANCE RECORDS.

a. Section 91.421 provides that zero time may be granted to an engine that has been rebuilt by a manufacturer or an agency approved by the manufacturer. When this is done, the owner/operator may use a new maintenance record without regard to previous operating history.

b. The manufacturer or an agency approved by the manufacturer that rebuilds and grants zero time to an engine is required by section 91.421 to provide a signed statement containing: 1) the date the engine was rebuilt; 2) each change made, as required by an AD; and 3) each change made in compliance with service bulletins, when the service bulletin specifically requests an entry to be made.

c. Section 43.2(b) prohibits the use of the term rebuilt in describing work accomplished in required maintenance records or forms unless the component worked on has had specific work functions accomplished. These functions are listed in section 43.2(b) and, except for testing requirements, are the same as those set forth in section 91.421(c). When terms such as remanufactured, reconditioned, or other terms coined by various aviation enterprises are used in maintenance records, owners and operators cannot assume that the functions outlined in section 43.2(b) have been done.

8. RECORDING TACHOMETERS.

a. Time-in-service recording devices sense such things as electrical power on, oil pressure, wheels on the ground, etc., and from these conditions provide an indication of time-in-service. With the exception of those that sense aircraft lift-off and touchdown, the indications are approximate.

b. Some owners and operators mistakenly believe these devices may be used in lieu of keeping time-in-service in the maintenance record. While they are of great assistance in arriving at the time-in-service, such instruments, alone, do not meet the requirements of section 91.417. For example, when the device fails and requires change, it is necessary to enter time-in-service and the instrument reading at the change. Otherwise, record continuity is lost.

9. MAINTENANCE RECORDS FOR AD COMPLIANCE.
This subject is covered in AC 39-7, Airworthiness Directives for General Aviation Aircraft, current edition. A separate AD record may be kept for the airframe and each engine, propeller, rotor, and appliance, but is not required. This would facilitate record searches when inspection is needed, and when an engine, propeller, rotor, or appliance is removed, the record may be transferred with it. Such records may also be used as a schedule for recurring inspections. The format, shown in Appendix 1, is a suggested one and adherence is not mandatory. Owners should be aware that they may be responsible for non-compliance with AD's when their aircraft are leased to foreign operators. They should, therefore, ensure that leases should be drafted to deal with this subject.

10. MAINTENANCE RECORDS FOR REQUIRED INSPECTIONS.

a. Section 43.11 contains the requirements for inspection entries. While these requirements are imposed on maintenance personnel, owners and operators should become familiar with them in order to meet their responsibilities under section 91.405.

b. The maintenance record requirements of section 43.11 apply to the 100-hour, annual, and progressive inspections under part 91; inspection programs under parts 91 and 125; approved airplane inspection programs under part 135; and the 100-hour and annual inspections under section 135.411(a)(1).

c. Appropriately rated mechanics are authorized to conduct these inspections and make the required entries. Particular attention should be given to section 43.11(a)(7) in that it now requires a more specific statement than previously required under section 43.9. The entry, in addition to other items, must identify the inspection program used; identify the portion or segment of the inspection program accomplished; and contain a statement that the inspection was performed in accordance with the instructions and procedures for that program.

d. Questions continue regarding multiple entries for 100-hour/annual inspections. As discussed in paragraph 5c, neither part 43 nor part 91 requires separate records to be kept. Section 43.11, however, requires persons approving or disapproving equipment for return to service, after any required inspection, to make an entry in the record of <u>that</u> equipment. Therefore, when an owner maintains a single record, the entry of the 100-hour or annual inspection is made in that record. If the owner maintains separate records for the airframe, powerplants, and propellers, the entry for the 100-hour inspection is entered in each, while the annual inspection is only required to be entered into the airframe record.

11. DISCREPANCY LISTS.

a. Before to October 15, 1982, issuance of discrepancy lists (or lists of defects) to owners or operators was appropriate only in connection with annual inspections under part 91; inspections under section 135.411(a)(1); inspection programs under part 125; and inspections under section 91.217. Now, section 43.11 requires that a discrepancy list be prepared by a person performing any inspection required by parts 91, 125, or section 135.411(a)(1).

b. When a discrepancy list is provided to an owner or operator, it says in effect, <u>except for these discrepancies, the item inspected is airworthy</u>. It is imperative, therefore, that inspections be complete and that all discrepancies appear in the list. When circumstances dictate that an inspection be terminated before it is completed, the maintenance record should clearly indicate that the inspection was discontinued. The entry should meet all the other requirements of section 43.11.

c. It is no longer a requirement that copies of discrepancy lists be forwarded to the local Flight Standards District Office (FSDO).

d. Discrepancy lists (or lists of defects) are part of the maintenance record and the owner/operator is responsible to maintain that record in accordance with section 91.417(b)(3) The entry made by maintenance personnel in the maintenance record should reference the discrepancy list when a list is issued.

12. LOST OR DESTROYED RECORDS.
Occasionally, the records for an aircraft are lost or destroyed. In order to re-construct them, it is necessary to establish the total time-in-service of the airframe. This can be done by reference to other records that reflect the time-in-service;

research of records maintained by repair facilities; and reference to records maintained by individual mechanics, etc. When these things have been done and the record is still incomplete, the owner/operator may make a notarized statement in the new record describing the loss and establishing the time-in-service based on the research and the best estimate of time-in-service.

a. The current status of applicable AD's may present a more formidable problem. This may require a detailed inspection by maintenance personnel to establish that the applicable AD's have been complied with. It can readily be seen that this could entail considerable time, expense, and in some instances, might require recompliance with the AD.

b. Other items required by section 91.417(a)(2), such as the current status of life-limited parts, time since last overhaul, current inspection status, and current list of major alterations, may present difficult problems. Some items may be easier to reestablish than others, but all are problems. Losing maintenance records can be troublesome, costly, and time consuming. Safekeeping of the records is an integral part of a good record keeping system.

13. COMPUTERIZED RECORDS. There is a growing trend toward computerized maintenance records. Many of these systems are offered to owners/operators on a commercial basis. While these are excellent scheduling systems, alone they normally do not meet the requirements of sections 43.9 or 91.417. The owner/operator who uses such a system is required to ensure that it provides the information required by section 91.417, including signatures. If not, modification to make them complete is the owner's/operator's responsibility and that responsibility may not be delegated.

14. PUBLIC AIRCRAFT. Prospective purchasers of aircraft that have been used as public aircraft, should be aware that public aircraft may not be subject to the certification and maintenance requirements in Title 14 of the Code of Federal Regulations and may not have records that meet the requirements of section 91.417. Considerable research may be involved in establishing the required records when these aircraft are purchased and brought into civil aviation. The aircraft may not be certificated or used without such records.

15. LIFE-LIMITED PARTS.

a. Present day aircraft and powerplants commonly have life-limited parts installed. These life limits may be referred to as retirement times, service life limitations, parts retirement limitations, retirement life limits, life limitations, or other such terminology and may be expressed in hours, cycles of operation, or calendar time. They are set forth in type certificate data sheets (TCDS), AD's, or the limitations section of FAA-approved airplane or rotorcraft flight manuals. Additionally, instructions for continued airworthiness, which require life-limits be specified, may apply (See CFR 23 Appendix G and CFR 27 Appendix A).

b. Section 91.417(a)(2)(ii) requires the owner or operator of an aircraft with such parts installed to have records containing the current status of these parts. Many owners/operators have found it advantageous to have a separate record for such parts showing the name of the part, part number, serial number, date of installation, total time-in-service, date removed, and signature and certificate number of the person installing or removing the part. A separate record, as described, facilitates transferring the record with the part in the event the part is removed and later reinstalled or installed on another aircraft or engine. If a separate record is not kept, the aircraft record must contain sufficient information to clearly establish the status of the life-limited parts installed.

16. MAINTENANCE RELEASE.

a. In addition to those requirements discussed previously, section 43.9 requires that major repairs and alterations be recorded as indicated in appendix B of part 43, (i.e., on FAA Form 337). An exception is provided in paragraph (b) of that appendix, which allows repair stations certificated under part 145 to use a maintenance release in lieu of the form for major repairs (and only major repairs).

b. The maintenance release must contain the information specified in paragraph (b)(1), (2) and (3), appendix B of part 43, be made a part of the aircraft maintenance record, and retained by the owner/operator as specified in section 91.417. The maintenance release is usually a special document (normally a tag) and is attached to the product when it is approved for return to service. The maintenance release may, however, be on a copy of the work order written for the product. When this is done (**for major repairs only**) the entry on the work order must meet paragraph (b)(1), (2), and (3) of the appendix. That is to say that the Repair Station is required to give the owner: (1) the customers work order upon which the repair is recorded; (2) a signed copy of the work order; and (3) a maintenance release which has been signed by an authorized representative of the company. In some cases, a work order and a maintenance release may be a different document. Both must be supplied to the customer.

c. Some repair stations use what they call a maintenance release for other than major repairs. This is sometimes a tag and sometimes information on a work order. When this is done, all of the requirements of section 43.9 must be met (paragraph (b)(3), appendix B, not applicable) and the document is to be made and retained as part of the maintenance records under section 91.417 per discussion in paragraph 5c.

17. FAA FORM 337, MAJOR REPAIR AND ALTERATION.

a. Major repairs and alterations are to be recorded on FAA Form 337, as stated in paragraph 16. This form is executed by the person making the repair or alteration. Provisions are made on the form for a person other than that person performing the work to approve the repair or alteration for return to service.

b. These forms are now required to be made part of the maintenance record of the product repaired or altered and retained in accordance with section 91.417.

c. Detailed instructions for use of this form are contained in AC 43.9-1, Instructions for Completion of FAA Form 337, current edition.

d. Some manufacturers have initiated a policy of indicating, on their service letters and bulletins, and other documents dealing with changes to their aircraft, whether or not the changes constitute major repairs or alterations. Some manufacturers also indicate that the responsibility for completing FAA Form 337 lies with the person accomplishing the repairs or alterations and cannot be delegated. When there is a question, it is advisable to contact the local FSDO for guidance.

18. TESTS AND INSPECTIONS FOR ALTIMETER SYSTEMS, ALTITUDE REPORTING EQUIPMENT, AND AIR TRAFFIC CONTROL (ATC) TRANSPONDERS.
The recordation requirements for these tests and inspections are the same as for other maintenance. There are essentially three tests and inspections (the altimeter system, the transponder system, and the data correspondence test), each of which may be subdivided relative to who may perform specific portions of the test. The basic authorization for performing these tests and inspections, found in section 43 3, is supplemented by sections 91.411 and 91.413. When multiple persons are involved in the performance of tests and inspections, care must be exercised to insure proper authorization under these three sections and compliance with sections 43.9 and 43.9(a)(3) in particular.

19. BEFORE YOU BUY.
This is the proper time to take a close look at the maintenance records of any used aircraft you expect to purchase. A well-kept set of maintenance records, which properly identifies all previously performed maintenance, alterations, and AD compliances, is generally a good indicator of the aircraft condition. This is not always the case, but in any event, before you buy, require the owner to produce the maintenance records for your examination, and require correction of any discrepancies found on the aircraft or in the records. Many prospective owners have found it advantageous to have a reliable unbiased maintenance person examine the maintenance records, as well as the aircraft, before negotiations have progressed too far. If the aircraft is purchased, take the time to review and learn the system of the previous owner to ensure compliance and continuity when you modify or continue that system.

Thomas E. Stuckey
Acting Director, Flight Standards
 Service

APPENDIX 1. AIRWORTHINESS DIRECTIVE COMPLIANCE RECORD (SUGGESTED FORMAT)

AD Number and Amendment Number	Date Received	Subject	Compliance Due Date Hours/Other	Date of Compliance	Airframe Total Time-in-Service at Compliance	One-Time	Recurring	Next Compliance Due Date Hours/Other	Authorized Signature, Certificate, Type and Number	Remarks

* Aircraft, Engine, Propeller, Rotor, or Appliance: Make _____ Model _____ S.N. _____ N _____

APPENDIX F

U.S. Department of Transportation
Federal Aviation Administration

Advisory Circular

Subject: INSTRUCTIONS FOR COMPLETION OF FAA FORM 337 (OMB NO. 2120-0020), MAJOR REPAIR AND ALTERATION (AIRFRAME, POWERPLANT, PROPELLER, OR APPLIANCE)

Date: 5/21/87
Initiated by: AFS-340

AC No: 43.9-1E
Change:

1. PURPOSE. This advisory circular (AC) provides instructions for completing Federal Aviation Administration (FAA) Form 337, Major Repair and Alteration (Airframe, Powerplant, Propeller, or Appliance).

2. CANCELLATION. AC 43.9-1D, Instructions for Completion of FAA Form 337 (OMB 04-R0060), Major Repair and Alteration (Airframe, Powerplant, Propeller, or Appliance), dated 9/5/79, is canceled.

3. RELATED FEDERAL AVIATION REGULATIONS (FAR) SECTIONS. FAR Part 43, Sections 43.5, 43.7, 43.9, and Appendix B.

4. INFORMATION. FAA Form 337 is furnished free of charge and is available at all FAA Air Carrier (ACDO), General Aviation (GADO), Manufacturing Inspection (MIDO), and Flight Standards (FSDO) district offices, and at all International Field Offices (IFO). The form serves two main purposes; one is to provide aircraft owners and operators with a record of major repairs or alterations indicating details and approval, and the other is to provide the FAA with a copy of the form for inclusion in the aircraft records at the FAA Aircraft Registration Branch, Oklahoma City, Oklahoma.

5. INSTRUCTIONS FOR COMPLETING FAA FORM 337. The person who performs or supervises a major repair or major alteration should prepare FAA Form 337. The form is executed at least in duplicate and is used to record major repairs and major alterations made to an aircraft, an airframe, powerplant, propeller, appliance, or spare part. The following instructions apply to corresponding items 1 through 8 of the form as illustrated in Appendix 1.

   a. Item 1 - Aircraft. Information to complete the "Make," "Model," and "Serial Number" blocks will be found on the aircraft manufacturer's identification plate. The "Nationality and Registration Mark" is the same as shown on AC Form 8050-3, Certificate of Aircraft Registration.

   b. Item 2 - Owner. Enter the aircraft owner's complete name and address as shown on AC Form 8050-3.

Note: When a major repair or alteration is made to a spare part or appliance, items 1 and 2 will be left blank, and the original and duplicate copy of the form will remain with the part until such time as it is installed on an aircraft. The person installing the part will then enter the required information in blocks 1 and 2, give the original of the form to the aircraft owner/operator, and forward the duplicate copy to the local FAA district office within 48 hours after the work is inspected.

   c. Item 3 - For FAA Use Only. Approval may be indicated in Item 3 when the FAA determines that data to be used in performing a major alteration or a major repair complies with accepted industry practices and all applicable FAR. Approval is indicated in one of the following methods. (See paragraph 6b for further details.)

      (1) Approval by examination of data only - one aircraft only: "The data identified herein complies with the applicable airworthiness requirements and is approved for the above described aircraft, subject to conformity inspection by a person authorized in FAR Part 43, Section 43.7."

      (2) Approval by physical inspection, demonstration, testing, etc., of the data and aircraft - one aircraft only: "The alteration (or repair) identified herein complies with the applicable airworthiness requirements and is approved for the above described aircraft, subject to conformity inspection by a person authorized in FAR Part 43, Section 43.7."

      (3) Approval by examination of data only - duplication on identical aircraft. "The alteration identified herein complies with the applicable airworthiness requirements and is approved for duplication on identical aircraft make, model, and altered configuration by the original modifier."

   d. 4 - Unit Identification. The information blocks under item 4 are used to identify the airframe, powerplant, propeller, or appliance repaired or altered. It is only necessary to complete the blocks for the unit repaired or altered.

   e. Item 5 - Type. Enter a checkmark in the appropriate column to indicate if the unit was repaired or altered.

   f. Item 6 - Conformity Statement.

      (1) "A" - Agency's Name and Address. Enter name of the mechanic, repair station, or manufacturer accomplishing the repair or alteration. Mechanics should enter their name and permanent mailing address. Manufacturers and repair stations should enter the name and address under which they do business.

      (2) "B" - Kind of Agency. Check the appropriate box to indicate the type of person or organization who performed the work.

(3) "C" - Certificate Number. Mechanics should enter their mechanic certificate number in this block, e.g., 1305888. Repair stations should enter their air agency certificate number and the rating or ratings under which the work was performed, e.g., 1234, Airframe Class 3. Manufacturers should enter their type production or Supplemental Type Certificate (STC) number. Manufacturers of Technical Standard Orders (TSO) appliances altering these appliances should enter the TSO number of the appliance altered.

(4) "D" - Compliance Statement: This space is used to certify that the repair or alteration was made in accordance with the FAR. When work was performed or supervised by certificated mechanics not employed by a manufacturer or repair station, they should enter the date the repair or alteration was completed and sign their full name. Repair stations are permitted to authorize persons in their employ to date and sign this conformity statement.

g. Item 7 - Approval for Return to Service. FAR Part 43 establishes the conditions under which major repairs or alterations to airframes, powerplants, propellers, and/or appliances may be approved for return to service. This portion of the form is used to indicate approval or rejection of the repair or alteration of the unit involved and to identify the person or agency making the airworthiness inspection. Check the "approved" or "rejected" box to indicate the finding. Additionally, check the appropriate box to indicate who made the finding. Use the box labeled "other" to indicate a finding by a person other than those listed. Enter the date the finding was made. The authorized person who made the finding should sign the form and enter the appropriate certificate or designation number.

h. Item 8 - Description of Work Accomplished. A clear, concise, and legible statement describing the work accomplished should be entered in item 8 on the reverse side of FAA Form 337. It is important that the location of the repair or alteration, relative to the aircraft or component, be described. The approved data used as the basis for approving the major repair or alteration for return to service should be identified and described in this area.

(1) For example, if a repair was made to a buckled spar, the description entered in this part might begin by stating, "Removed wing from aircraft and removed skin from outer 6 feet. Repaired buckled spar 49 inches from tip in accordance with . . . ." and continue with a description of the repair. The description should refer to applicable FAR sections and to the FAA-approved data used to substantiate the airworthiness of the repair or alteration. If the repair or alteration is subject to

being covered by skin or other structure, a statement should be made certifying that a precover inspection was made and that covered areas were found satisfactory.

(2) <u>Data used</u> as a basis for approving major repairs or alterations for return to service must be FAA-approved prior to its use for that purpose and includes: FAR (e.g., airworthiness directives), AC's (e.g., AC 43.13-1A under certain circumstances), TSO's parts manufacturing approval (PMA), FAA-approved manufacturer's instructions, kits and service handbooks, type certificate data sheets, and aircraft specifications. Other forms of approved data would be those approved by a designated engineering representative (DER), a manufacturer holding a delegation option authorization (DOA), STC's, and, with certain limitations, previous FAA field approvals. Supporting data such as stress analyses, test reports, sketches, or photographs should be submitted with the FAA Form 337. These supporting data will be returned to the applicant by the local FAA district office since only FAA Form 337 is retained as a part of the aircraft records at Oklahoma City.

(3) <u>If additional space is needed</u> to describe the repair or alteration, attach sheets bearing the aircraft nationality and registration mark and the date work was completed.

(4) <u>Showing weight and balance computations</u> under this item is not required; however, it may be done. In all cases where weight and balance of the aircraft are affected, the changes should be entered in the aircraft weight and balance records with the date, signature, and reference to the work performed on the FAA Form 337 that required the changes.

6. <u>ADMINISTRATIVE PROCESSING</u>. At least an original and one duplicate copy of the FAA Form 337 will be executed. FAA district office processing of the forms and their supporting data will depend upon whether previously approved or non-previously approved data was used as follows:

a. <u>Previously Approved Data</u>. The forms will be completed as instructed in this AC ensuring that item 7, "Approval for Return to Service," has been properly executed. Give the original of the form to the aircraft owner or operator, and send the duplicate copy to the local FAA district office within 48 hours after the work is inspected.

b. <u>Non-previously Approved Data</u>. The forms will be completed as instructed in this AC, leaving item 7, "Approval for Return to Service," blank. Both copies of the form, with supporting data, will be sent to the local FAA district office. When the FAA determines that the major repair or alteration data complies with applicable regulations and is in conformity with accepted industry practices, data approval will be recorded by entering an appropriate statement in item 3, "For FAA Use Only." Both forms and supporting data will be returned to the applicant who will complete item 7, "Approval for Return to Service." The applicant will give the original of the form, with its supporting data, to the aircraft owner or operator and return the duplicate copy to the local FAA district office who will, in turn, forward it to the FAA Aircraft Registration Branch, Oklahoma City, Oklahoma, for inclusion in the aircraft records.

c. **Signatures on FAA Form 337** have limited purposes:

(1) A signature in item 3, "For FAA Use Only," indicates approval of the data described in that section for use in accomplishing the work described under item 8 on the reverse of FAA Form 337.

(2) A signature in item 6, "Conformity Statement," is a certification by the person performing the work that it was accomplished in accordance with applicable FAR and FAA-approved data. The certification is only applicable to that work described under item 8 on the reverse of FAA Form 337.

Note: Neither of these signatures (subparagraph c(1) and c(2)) indicate FAA approval of the work described under item 8 for return to service.

(3) A signature in item 7, "Approval for Return to Service," does not signify FAA approval unless the box to the left of "FAA Flight Standards Inspector" or "FAA Designee" is checked. The other persons listed in item 7, are authorized to "approve for return to service" if the repair or alteration is accomplished using FAA-approved data, is performed in accordance with applicable FAR, and found to conform.

d. **FAA Form 337 is not authorized** for use on other than U.S.-registered aircraft. If a foreign civil air authority requests the form, as a record of work performed, it may be provided. The form should be executed in accordance with the FAR and this AC. The foreign authority should be notified on the form that it is not an official record and that it will not be recorded by the FAA Aircraft Registration Branch, Oklahoma City, Oklahoma.

e. **FAR Part 43, Appendix B, Paragraph (b)** authorizes FAA certificated repair stations to use a work order, in lieu of FAA Form 337, for **only major repairs**. Such work orders should contain all the information provided on the form and in no less detail; that is, the data used as a basis of approval should be identified, a certification that the work was accomplished using that data and in accordance with the FAR, a description of the work performed (as required in item 8 of the FAA Form 337), and approval for return to service must be indicated by an authorized person. Signature, kind of certificate, and certificate number must also appear in the record (reference FAR Section 43.9).

William T. Brennan
Acting Director of Flight Standards

5/21/87

AC 43.9-1E
Appendix 1

APPENDIX 1. FAA FORM 337 (FRONT), MAJOR REPAIR AND ALTERATION (AIRFRAME, POWERPLANT, PROPELLER, OR APPLIANCE)

MAJOR REPAIR AND ALTERATION
(Airframe, Powerplant, Propeller, or Appliance)

US Department of Transportation
Federal Aviation Administration

Form Approved
OMB No. 2120-0020

For FAA Use Only
Office Identification

INSTRUCTIONS: Print or type all entries. See FAR 43.9, FAR 43 Appendix B, and AC 43.9-1 (or subsequent revision thereof) for instructions and disposition of this form. This report is required by law (49 U.S.C. 1421). Failure to report can result in a civil penalty not to exceed $1,000 for each such violation (Section 901 Federal Aviation Act of 1958).

1. Aircraft
- Make: Cessna
- Model: 182
- Serial No: 15-10521
- Nationality and Registration Mark: N-3763

2. Owner
- Name (As shown on registration certificate): William Taylor
- Address (As shown on registration certificate): 36 Main Street, Cambria, Pennsylvania 15946

3. For FAA Use Only

The data identified herein complies with the applicable airworthiness requirements and is approved for the above described aircraft, subject to conformity inspection by a person authorized by FAR Part 43. *Ralph Burlingame*

AEA-GADO-19 — District Office
April 5, 1986 — Date
Signature of FAA Inspector: Ralph Burlingame

4. Unit Identification | **5. Type**

Unit	Make	Model	Serial No	Repair	Alteration
AIRFRAME	(As described in Item 1 above)			X	
POWERPLANT					
PROPELLER					
APPLIANCE (Type / Manufacturer)					

6. Conformity Statement

A. Agency's Name and Address:
George Morris
High Street
Johnstown, Pennsylvania 15236

B. Kind of Agency:
[X] U.S. Certificated Mechanic
[ ] Foreign Certificated Mechanic
[ ] Certificated Repair Station
[ ] Manufacturer

C. Certificate No: 1305888

D. I certify that the repair and/or alteration made to the unit(s) identified in item 4 above and described on the reverse or attachments hereto have been made in accordance with the requirements of Part 43 of the U.S. Federal Aviation Regulations and that the information furnished herein is true and correct to the best of my knowledge.

Date: March 19, 1987
Signature of Authorized Individual: George Morris

7. Approval for Return To Service

Pursuant to the authority given persons specified below, the unit identified in item 4 was inspected in the manner prescribed by the Administrator of the Federal Aviation Administration and is [X] APPROVED [ ] REJECTED

BY:
[ ] FAA Flt Standards Inspector
[ ] Manufacturer
[X] Inspection Authorization
[ ] FAA Designee
[ ] Repair Station
[ ] Person Approved by Transport Canada Airworthiness Group
[ ] Other (Specify)

Date of Approval or Rejection: April 9, 1987
Certificate or Designation No: 237412
Signature of Authorized Individual: Donald Pauley

FAA Form 337 (4-87)

FAA FORM 337 (BACK), MAJOR REPAIR AND ALTERATION (AIRFRAME, POWERPLANT, PROPELLER, OR APPLIANCE)

NOTICE

Weight and balance or operating limitation changes shall be entered in the appropriate aircraft record. An alteration must be compatible with all previous alterations to assure continued conformity with the applicable airworthiness requirements.

---

8. Description of Work Accomplished
(If more space is required, attach additional sheets. Identify with aircraft nationality and registration mark and date work completed.)

1. Removed right wing from aircraft and removed skin from outer 6 feet. Repaired buckled spar 49 inches from tip in accordance with attached photographs and figure 1 of drawing dated March 6, 1987.

    DATE: March 15, 1987, inspected splice in Item 1 and found it to be in accordance with data indicated. Splice is okay to cover. Inspected internal and external wing assembly for hidden damage and condition.

    Donald Pauley

    Donald Pauley, A&P 237412 IA

2. Primed interior wing structure and replaced skin P/Ns 63-0085, 63-0086, and 63-00878 with same material, 2024-T3, .025 inches thick. Rivet size and spacing all the same as original and using procedures in Chapter 2, Section 3, of AC 43.13-1A, dated 1972.

3. Replaced stringers as required and installed 6 splices as per attached drawing and photographs.

4. Installed wing, rigged aileron, and operationally checked in accordance with manufacturer's maintenance manual.

5. No change in weight or balance.

END

☐ Additional Sheets Are Attached

APPENDIX G

U.S. Department
of Transportation
**Federal Aviation
Administration**

Advisory Circular

Subject: **AIRWORTHINESS DIRECTIVES** Date: 11/16/95 AC No: **39-7C**
Initiated by: **AFS-340** Change:

---

1. PURPOSE. This advisory circular (AC) provides guidance and information to owners and operators of aircraft concerning their responsibility for complying with airworthiness directives (AD) and recording AD compliance in the appropriate maintenance records.

2. CANCELLATION. AC 39-7B, Airworthiness Directives, dated April 8, 1987, is canceled.

3. PRINCIPAL CHANGES. References to specific Federal Aviation Regulations have been updated and text reworded for clarification throughout this document.

4. RELATED FEDERAL AVIATION REGULATIONS. 14 Code of Federal Regulations (CFR) part 39; part 43, §§ 43.9 and 43.11; part 91, §§ 91.403, 91.417, and 91.419.

5. BACKGROUND. The authority for the role of the Federal Aviation Administration (FAA) regarding the promotion of safe flight for civil aircraft may be found generally at Title 49 of the United State Code (USC) § 44701 et. seq. (formerly, Title VI of the Federal Aviation Act of 1958 and related statutes). One of the ways the FAA has implemented its authority is through 14 CFR part 39, Airworthiness Directives. Pursuant to its authority, the FAA issues AD's when an unsafe condition is found to exist in a product (aircraft, aircraft engine, propeller, or appliance) of a particular type design. AD's are used by the FAA to notify aircraft owners and operators of unsafe conditions and to require their correction. AD's prescribe the conditions and limitations, including inspection, repair, or alteration under which the product may continue to be operated. AD's are authorized under part 39 and issued in accordance with the public rulemaking procedures of the Administrative Procedure Act, 5 USC 553, and FAA procedures in part 11.

6. AD CATEGORIES. AD's are published in the Federal Register as amendments to part 39. Depending on the urgency, AD's are issued as follows:

   a. Normally a notice of proposed rulemaking (NPRM) for an AD is issued and published in the Federal Register when an unsafe condition is found to exist in a product. Interested persons are invited to comment on the NPRM by submitting such written data, views, contained in the notice may be changed or withdrawn in light of comments received. When the final rule, resulting from the NPRM, is adopted, it is published in the Federal Register, printed and distributed by first class mail to the registered owners and certain known operators of the product(s) affected.

   b. Emergency AD's. AD's of an urgent nature may be adopted without prior notice (without an NPRM) under emergency procedures as immediately adopted rules. The AD's normally become effective in less than 30 days after publication in the Federal Register and are distributed by first class mail, telegram, or other electronic methods to the registered owners and certain known operators of the product affected. In addition, notification is also provided to special interest groups, other government agencies, and Civil Aviation Authorities of certain foreign countries.

7. AD's WHICH APPLY TO PRODUCTS OTHER THAN AIRCRAFT. AD's may be issued which apply to aircraft engines, propellers, or appliances installed on multiple makes or models of aircraft. When the product can be identified as being installed on a specific make or model aircraft, the AD is distributed by first class mail to the registered owners of those aircraft. However, there are times when such a determination cannot be made, and direct distribution to registered owners is impossible. For this reason, aircraft owners and operators are urged to subscribe to the Summary of Airworthiness Directives which contains all previously published AD's and a biweekly supplemental service. Advisory Circular 39-6, Announcement of Availability--Summary of Airworthiness Directives, provides ordering information and subscription prices on these publications. The most recent copy of AC 39-6 may be obtained, without cost, from the U.S. Department of Transportation, General Services Section, M-483.1, Washington, D.C. 20590. Information concerning the Summary of Airworthiness Directives may also be obtained by contacting the FAA, Manufacturing Standards Section (AFS-613), P.O. Box 26460, Oklahoma City, Oklahoma 73125-0460. Telephone (405) 954-4103, FAX (405) 954-4104.

8. APPLICABILITY OF AD's. Each AD contains an applicability statement specifying the product (aircraft, aircraft engine, propeller, or appliance) to which it applies. Some aircraft owners and operators mistakenly assume that AD's do not apply to aircraft with other than standard airworthiness certificates, i.e., special airworthiness certificates in the restricted, limited, or experimental category. Unless specifically stated, AD's apply to the make and model set forth in the applicability statement regardless of the classification or category of the airworthiness certificate issued for the aircraft. Type certificate and airworthiness certification information are used to identify the product affected. Limitations may be placed on applicability by specifying the serial number or number series to which the AD is applicable. When there is no reference to serial numbers, all serial numbers are affected. The following are examples of AD applicability statements:

   a. "Applies to Smith (Formerly Robin Aero) RA-15-150 series airplanes, certificated in any category." This statement, or one similarly worded, makes the AD applicable to all airplanes of the model listed, regardless of the type of airworthiness certificate issued to the aircraft.

b. "Applies to Smith (Formerly Robin Aero) RA-15-150 Serial Numbers 15-1081 through 15-1098." This statement, or one similarly worded, specifies certain aircraft by serial number within a specific model and series regardless of the type of airworthiness certificate issued to the aircraft.

c. "Applies to Smith (Formerly Robin Aero) RA-15-150 series aircraft certificated in all categories excluding experimental aircraft." This statement, or one similarly worded, makes the AD applicable to all airplanes except those issued experimental airworthiness certificates.

d. "Applicability: Smith (Formerly Robin Aero) RA-15-150 series airplanes; Cessna Models 150, 170, 172, and 175 series airplanes; and Piper PA-28-140 airplanes; certificated in any category, that have been modified in accordance with STC SA807NM using ABLE INDUSTRIES, Inc., (Part No. 1234) muffler kits." This statement, or one similarly worded, makes the AD applicable to all airplanes listed when altered by the supplemental type certificate listed, regardless of the type of airworthiness certificate issued to the aircraft.

e. Every AD applies to each product identified in the applicability statement, regardless of whether it has been modified, altered, or repaired in the area subject to the requirements of the AD. For products that have been modified, altered, or repaired so that performance of the requirements of the AD is affected, the owner/operator must use the authority provided in the alternative methods of compliance provision of the AD (see paragraph 12) to request approval from the FAA. This approval may address either no action, if the current configuration eliminates the unsafe condition; or, different actions necessary to address the unsafe condition described in the AD. In no case, does the presence of any alteration, modification, or repair remove any product from the applicability of this AD. Performance of the requirements of the AD is "affected" if an operator is unable to perform those requirements in the manner described in the AD. In short, either the requirements of the AD can be performed as specified in the AD and the specified results can be achieved, or they cannot.

9. AD COMPLIANCE. AD's are regulations issued under part 39. Therefore, <u>no person may operate a product to which an AD applies, except in accordance with the requirements of that AD</u>. Owners and operators should understand that to "operate" not only means piloting the aircraft, but also causing or authorizing the product to be used for the purpose of air navigation, with or without the right of legal control as owner, lessee, or otherwise. Compliance with emergency AD's can be a problem for operators of leased aircraft because the FAA has no legal requirement for notification of other than registered owners. Therefore, it is important that the registered owner(s) of leased aircraft make the AD information available to the operators leasing their aircraft as expeditiously as possible, otherwise the lessee may not be aware of the AD and safety may be jeopardized.

10. COMPLIANCE TIME OR DATE.

a. The belief that AD compliance is only required at the time of a required inspection, e.g., at a 100-hour or annual inspection is <u>not correct</u>. The required compliance time is specified in each AD, and no person may operate the affected product after expiration of that stated compliance time.

b. Compliance requirements specified in AD's are established for safety reasons and may be stated in various ways. Some AD's are of such a serious nature they require compliance before further flight, for example: "To prevent uncommanded engine shutdown with the inability to restart the engine, prior to further flight, inspect...." Other AD's express compliance time in terms of a specific number of hours in operation, for example: "Compliance is required within the next 50 hours time in service after the effective date of this AD." Compliance times may also be expressed in operational terms, such as: "Within the next 10 landings after the effective date of this AD...." For turbine engines, compliance times are often expressed in terms of cycles. A cycle normally consists of an engine start, takeoff operation, landing, and engine shutdown.

c. When a direct relationship between airworthiness and calendar time is identified, compliance time may be expressed as a calendar date. For example, if the compliance time is specified as "within 12 months after the effective date of this AD...." with an effective date of July 15, 1995, the deadline for compliance is July 15, 1996.

d. In some instances, the AD may authorize flight after the compliance date has passed, provided that a special flight permit is obtained. Special flight authorization may be granted only when the AD specifically permits such operation. Another aspect of compliance times to be emphasized is that not all AD's have a one-time compliance requirement. Repetitive inspections at specified intervals after initial compliance may be required in lieu of, or until a permanent solution for the unsafe condition is developed.

11. ADJUSTMENTS IN COMPLIANCE REQUIREMENTS.
In some instances, a compliance time other than the compliance time specified in the AD may be advantageous to an aircraft owner or operator. In recognition of this need, and when an acceptable level of safety can be shown, flexibility may be provided by a statement in the AD allowing adjustment of the specified interval. When adjustment authority is provided in an AD, owners or operators desiring to make an adjustment are required to submit data substantiating their proposed adjustment to their local FAA Flight Standards District Office or other FAA office for consideration as specified in the AD. The FAA office or person authorized to approve adjustments in compliance requirements is normally identified in the AD.

12. ALTERNATIVE METHODS OF COMPLIANCE.
Many AD's indicate the acceptability of one or more alternative methods of compliance. <u>Any alternative</u> method of compliance or adjustment of compliance time other than that listed in the AD must be substantiated and approved by the FAA before it may be used. Normally the office or person authorized to approve an alternative method of compliance is indicated in the AD.

13. RESPONSIBILITY FOR AD COMPLIANCE AND RECORDATION. The <u>owner or operator of an aircraft is primarily responsible</u> for maintaining that aircraft in an airworthy condition, including compliance with AD's.

   a. This responsibility may be met by ensuring that properly certificated and appropriately rated maintenance person(s) accomplish the requirements of the AD and properly record this action in the appropriate maintenance records. This action must be accomplished within the compliance time specified in the AD or the aircraft may not be operated.

   b. Maintenance persons may also have direct responsibility for AD compliance, aside from the times when AD compliance is the specific work contracted for by the owner or operator. When a 100-hour, annual, progressive, or any other inspection required under parts 91, 121, 125, or 135 is accomplished, § 43.15 (a) requires the person performing the inspection to determine that <u>all</u> applicable airworthiness requirements are met, including compliance with AD's.

   c. Maintenance persons should note even though an inspection of the complete aircraft is not made, if the inspection conducted is a progressive inspection, determination of AD compliance is required for those portions of the aircraft inspected.

   d. For aircraft being inspected in accordance with a continuous inspection program (§ 91.409), the person performing the inspection must ensure that an AD is complied with only when the portion of the inspection program being handled by that person involves an area covered by a particular AD. The program may require a determination of AD compliance for the entire aircraft by a general statement, or compliance with AD's applicable only to portions of the aircraft being inspected, or it may not require compliance at all. This does not mean AD compliance is not required at the compliance time or date specified in the AD. It only means that the owner or operator has elected to handle AD compliance apart from the inspection program. <u>The owner or operator remains fully responsible for AD compliance</u>.

   e. The person accomplishing the AD is required by § 43.9 to record AD compliance. The entry must include those items specified in § 43.9 (a) (1) through (a) (4). The owner or operator is required by § 91.405 to ensure that maintenance personnel make appropriate entries and, by § 91.417, to maintain those records. Owners and operators should note that there is a difference between the records required to be kept by the owner under § 91.417 and those § 43.9 requires maintenance personnel to make. In either case, the owner or operator <u>is responsible</u> for maintaining proper records.

   f. <u>Pilot Performed AD Checks</u>. Certain AD's permit pilots to perform checks of some items under specific conditions. AD's allowing this action will include specific direction regarding recording requirements. However, if the AD does not include recording requirements for the pilot, § 43.9 requires persons complying with an AD to make an entry in the maintenance record of that product. § 91.417 (a) and (b) requires the <u>owner or operator</u> to keep and retain certain minimum records for a specific time. The person who accomplished the action, the person who returned the aircraft to service, and the status of AD compliance are the items of information required to be kept in those records.

14. RECURRING/PERIODIC AD's. Some AD's require repetitive or periodic inspection. In order to provide for flexibility in administering such AD's, an AD may provide for adjustment of the inspection interval to coincide with inspections required by part 91, or other regulations. The conditions and approval requirements under which adjustments may be allowed are stated in the AD. If the AD does not contain such provisions, adjustments are usually not permitted. However, amendment, modification, or adjustment of the terms of the AD may be requested by contacting the office that issued the AD or by following the petition procedures provided in part 11.

15. DETERMINING REVISION DATES. The revision date required by § 91.417 (a) (2) (v) is the effective date of the latest amendment to the AD and may be found in the last sentence of the body of each AD. For example: "This amendment becomes effective on July 10, 1995." Similarly, the revision date for an emergency AD distributed by telegram or priority mail is the date it was issued. For example: "Priority Letter AD 95-11-09, issued May 25, 1995, becomes effective upon receipt." Each emergency AD is normally followed by a final rule version that will reflect the final status and amendment number of the regulation including any changes in the effective date.

16. SUMMARY. The registered owner or operator of an aircraft is responsible for compliance with AD's applicable to the airframe, engine, propeller, appliances, and parts and components thereof for all aircraft it owns or operates. Maintenance personnel are responsible for determining that all applicable airworthiness requirements are met when they accomplish an inspection in accordance with part 43.

Thomas C. Accardi
Director, Flight Standards Service

APPENDIX H

U.S. Department of Transportation
Federal Aviation Administration

Advisory Circular

Subject: SERVICE DIFFICULTY PROGRAM (GENERAL AVIATION)	Date: 4/8/93 Initiated by: AFS-640	AC No: AC 20-109A Change:

1. **PURPOSE.** This advisory circular (AC) describes the Service Difficulty Program as it applies to general aviation activities. Instructions for completion of the revised FAA Form 8010-4 (10-92), Malfunction or Defect Report, are provided. This AC also solicits the participation of the aviation community in the Service Difficulty Program and their cooperation in improving the quality of FAA Form 8010-4.

2. **CANCELLATION.** AC 20-109, Service Difficulty Program (General Aviation), dated 1/8/79, is canceled.

3. **FORMS.** FAA Form 8010-4 (10-92), Malfunction or Defect Report, (National Stock Number (NSN) 0052-00-039-1005, Unit of Issue "BK" (25 forms per book), is available free from Flight Standards District Offices (FSDO's). See appendix 1 for directions on completing FAA Form 8010-4.

4. **DISCUSSION.** The Service Difficulty Program is an information system designed to provide assistance to aircraft owners, operators, maintenance organizations, manufacturers, and the Federal Aviation Administration (FAA) in identifying aircraft problems encountered during service. The Service Difficulty Program provides for the collection, organization, analysis, and dissemination of aircraft service information to improve service reliability of aeronautical products. The primary sources of this information are the aircraft maintenance facilities, owners, and operators. General aviation aircraft service difficulty information is normally submitted to the FAA by use of FAA Form 8010-4. However, information will be accepted in any form or format when FAA Form 8010-4 is not readily available for use.

5. **INPUT.** All of the FAA Forms 8010-4 are received by local FSDO's or Certificate Management Offices (CMO's). All the FAA Forms 8010-4 are reviewed for immediate impact items, and then forwarded for processing to the Flight Standards Service, Safety Data Analysis Section (AFS-643), in Oklahoma City, Oklahoma.

The information contained in the FAA Form 8010-4 is stored in a computerized data bank for retrieval and analysis. Items potentially hazardous to flight are telephoned directly to AFS-643 personnel by FAA Aviation Safety Inspectors in FSDO's. These items are immediately referred to, and expeditiously handled by, the appropriate FAA offices.

   a. **Certain owners, operators, certificate holders, and certificated repair stations are required by the Federal Aviation Regulations (FAR) to submit reports of defects, unairworthy conditions, and mechanical reliability problems to the FAA.** However, success of the Service Difficulty Program is enhanced by submission of service difficulty information by all of the aviation community regardless of whether required by regulation. Voluntary submission of service difficulty information is strongly encouraged.

   b. **Additional service difficulty information is collected by FAA Aviation Safety Inspectors** in the performance of routine aircraft and maintenance surveillance, accident and incident investigations, during the operation of rental aircraft, and during pilot certification flights.

AC 20-109A   4/8/93

    c.   **All service difficulty information is retained in the computer data bank** for a period of 5 years providing a base for the detection of trends and failure rates. If necessary, data in excess of 5 years may be retrieved through the archives.

6.   **THE INFORMATION MANAGEMENT SECTION, AFS-624, IS AN INFORMATION CENTER.** AFS-624 personnel responds to individual requests from the aviation community concerning service difficulty information. Further details regarding computer-generated service difficulty information, may be obtained by telephoning (405) 954-4173 or by writing to:

>   FAA
>   Flight Standards Service
>   **ATTN: Information Management Section (AFS-624)**
>   P.O. Box 25082
>   Oklahoma City, OK 73125-5012

7.   **PUBLICATIONS PRODUCED BY AFS-643.** Analysis of service difficulty information is primarily done by AFS-643. When trends are detected, they are made available to pertinent FAA field personnel for their information and possible investigation. AFS-643 produces the following publications.

    a.   **The Flight Standards Service Difficulty Reports (General and Commercial),** known as the weekly summary, contains all information obtained from FAA Forms 8010-4 and those service difficulties which were reported by telephone. Reports of a significant nature are highlighted with a "star" border, while reports which are of an "URGENT AIRWORTHINESS CONCERN" are highlighted with a "black and white slashed" border. These highly significant items are sometimes obtained from sources other than FAA Forms 8010-4. This publication is distributed to FSDO's, Manufacturing Inspection District Offices (MIDO's), and Aircraft Certification Offices (ACO's). This publication is also made available to the public free of charge by telephoning (405) 954-4171 or by writing to AFS-643 at the following address:

>   FAA
>   Flight Standards Service
>   **ATTN: Safety Data Analysis Section (AFS-643)**
>   P.O. Box 25082
>   Oklahoma City, OK 73125-5029

    b.   **AC 43-16, General Aviation Airworthiness Alerts,** contains information that is of assistance to maintenance and inspection personnel in the performance of their duties. These items are developed from submitted FAA Form 8010-4 and articles pertaining to aviation. This publication is made available to the public free of charge by telephoning (405) 954-4171 or by writing to AFS-643 (see the address given in paragraph 7a).

8.   **IMPORTANCE OF REPORTING.** The FAA requests the cooperation of all aircraft owners, operators, mechanics, pilots, and others in reporting service difficulties experienced with airframes, powerplants, propellers, or appliances/components.

    a.   **FAA Forms 8010-4 provide the FAA and industry with a very essential service record** of mechanical difficulties encountered in aircraft operations. Such reports contribute to the correction of conditions or situations which otherwise will continue to prove costly and/or adversely affect the airworthiness of aircraft.

b. **When a system component or part of an aircraft (powerplants, propellers, or appliances) functions badly or fails to operate in the normal or usual manner,** it has malfunctioned and should be reported. Also, if a system, component, or part has a flaw or imperfection which impairs function or which may impair future function, it is defective and should be reported. While at first sight it appears this will generate numerous insignificant reports, the Service Difficulty Program is designed to detect trends. Any report can be very constructive in evaluating design or maintenance reliability.

c. **When preparing FAA Form 8010-4,** furnish as much information as possible. Any attachments such as photographs and sketches of defective parts are appreciated. However, do not send parts to AFS-643. AFS-643 does not have storage facilities for defective parts.

d. **Public cooperation in submitting service difficulty information is greatly appreciated** by the FAA and others who have an interest in safety. The quantity of service difficulty reports received precludes individual acknowledgement of each report.

Thomas C. Accardi
Director, Flight Standards Service

4/8/93
AC 20-109A
Appendix 1

Appendix 1. INSTRUCTIONS FOR COMPLETING THE REVISED FAA FORM 8010-4 (10-92), MALFUNCTION OR DEFECT REPORT

H-4

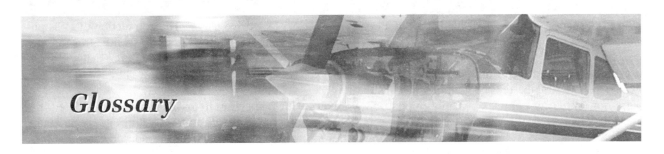

Glossary

This glossary of terms is provided to serve as a ready reference for the words with which you may not be familiar. These definitions may differ from those of standard dictionaries, but are in keeping with shop usage.

airworthiness directive A directive issued by the FAA to correct an unsafe condition that may exist on an aircraft and it must be complied with.

airworthy Safe for flight and meets all of the applicable requirements determined by the FAA and the manufacturer to be necessary for flying the aircraft.

annual inspection An inspection designed to determine if an aircraft is airworthy or unairworthy.

appliance Any instrument, mechanism, equipment, part, apparatus, appurtenance, or accessory, including communications equipment, that is used or intended to be used in operating or controlling an aircraft in flight, is installed in or attached to the aircraft, and is not part of an airframe, engine, or propeller.

applicability Something that applies to and/or affects another.

approved This term has two definitions in this publication:

(1) that a mechanic has approved or stated the aircraft has met all applicable airworthiness requirements and is ready for flight; (2) that the information is approved by the FAA such as found on the back of the Form 337.

approved inspection system A maintenance program consisting of the inspection and maintenance necessary to maintain an aircraft in airworthy condition.

authorized Being given the legal right to perform certain functions by the FAA.

calendar month A time period that expires on the last day of the month irregardless on what day the month it begins.

certificate An official FAA document authorizing a privilege, fact, or legal concept.

compliance To accomplish as required by regulation or directive.

conformity Meeting all of the requirements of its original or properly altered conditions as specified in the Type Certificate Data Sheets and the manufacturer's specification.

continuous airworthiness program A maintenance program consisting of the inspection and maintenance necessary to maintain an aircraft or a fleet of aircraft in airworthy condition and is usually used on large or turbine powered aircraft.

designated Being given the legal right and authority to perform certain specified functions by the FAA.

detailed inspection item An inspection item of a progressive inspection may involve disassembly to inspect and could even be to overhaul a component or part.

ELT The common abbreviation for the emergency locator transmitter.

inspect The determination of the condition of something by sight, feel, measurement, or other methods.

inspection The determination of the condition of something by sight, feel, measurement, or other means.

life-limited part A part or component that has a designated number of hours or calendar time in service after which it will be replaced and is not longer usable.

maintenance release A return to service approval in the appropriate maintenance record.

major alteration A repair that if improperly done, might appreciably affect weight, balance, structural strength, performance, powerplant operation, flight characteristics, or other qualities affecting airworthiness, or that is not done according to accepted practices or cannot be done by elementary operations and is not included in Type Certificate Data Sheets or manufacturer's specification for the aircraft.

major repair A repair that if improperly done, might appreciably affect weight, balance, structural strength, performance, powerplant operation, flight characteristics, or other qualities affecting airworthiness, or that is not done according to accepted practices or cannot be done by elementary operations.

phase A section or a distinguishable part of a maintenance program or inspection.

preventive maintenance Simple or minor preservative operations and the replacement of small standard parts not involving complex assembly operation as listed in Appendix A of FAR 43.

recurring An airworthiness directive that requires compliance at regular hourly or calendar time periods.

return to service The completion of all applicable maintenance records and forms after maintenance has been performed on an aircraft that will allow the aircraft to be legally flown.

routine inspection items Inspection items listed in a progressive inspection that require only a visual inspection to determine their condition.

time-in-service The time from the moment an aircraft leaves the surface of the earth until it touches down at the next point of landing.

ANSWERS TO STUDY QUESTIONS

AIRCRAFT MAINTENANCE AND INSPECTION RECORDS

CHAPTER 1

1. If the aircraft has been inspected by an IA and found to be unairworthy, an A&P mechanic can repair the discrepancies and approve the aircraft for return to service if the repairs are preventive or minor in nature.

2. Pilot in command (PIC)

3. Yes, if they hold at least a private pilot certificate, and have previous experience doing the work.

4. Yes. If the flight is to relocate the aircraft to a place where the inspection can be performed, up to 10 hours may be flown beyond the inspection due time.

5. False. The A&P must hold both ratings for a minimum of three years, and then they must take the required tests to obtain an Inspection Authorization from the FAA.

6. Radio Rating, Class 1.

CHAPTER 2

1. An A&P technician or an authorized representative of a certified repair station if all the maintenance items repaired are classified as a minor repair.

2. June 30th, 1994

3. Yes. A list of discrepancies must be provided to the owner or operator.

4. An A&P holding an Inspection Authorization (IA), an authorized representative of a certificated repair station, and the manufacturer of the aircraft.

5. Those aircraft flown for hire and those that are used for flight instruction for hire in an aircraft that the instructor provides.

6. Yes. With a special airworthiness certificate or ferry permit.

7. 10 hours.

8. An A&P Mechanic.

9. Less down time at one time for the aircraft.

CHAPTER 3

1. Volume 2

2. That the AD was the 5th AD issued in the 2nd biweekly revision cycle.

3. The date the AD was complied with, total time (as required), AD number, revision and amendment number, method of compliance by reference to the specific AD part or paragraph that was performed, one-time or recurring (including next due date or time if recurring), signature and certificate number of the person that complied with the AD.

4. The aircraft's equipment list.

5. When the service action is required as prescribed in an airworthiness directive.

CHAPTER 4

1. By a person's own design, manufacturers checklist, or 14 CFR Part 43, Appendix D

2. Maximum power RPM with the aircraft stationary or not moving.

3. Static and idle RPM, magnetos, fuel and oil pressures, cylinder and oil temperatures, all other operating systems for manufacturer's specifications.

4. Pre-inspection phase, look phase, service and repair phase, functional check phase, and return to service phase.

5. Look phase.

6. By completing the appropriate entries in the maintenance records with the signature and certificate number of the authorizing individual.

7. When required by regulations.

CHAPTER 5

1. Yes.

2. No.

3. Condition, cleanliness, TSO C22 printed on the identification tag, security of attachment, and operation of the latching mechanism.

An-1

4. Airworthiness certificate, registration certificate.

5. Proper installation, battery replacement date, antenna connection and condition, and operation including the activation system.

6. Water level and state of charge.

7. Retraction safety switch, excessive wear, proper operation, binding, chafing, up-lock operation, electrical switch operation, up-lock tension and clearance, up indicating system, gear warning horn operation, down-locks for proper operation and tension, down-lock indicating lights and switches, door operation and fit.

8. Oil screen and compression check.

9. Timing, breaker gap, and security.

CHAPTER 6

1. They can perform the major alteration or major repair but they cannot approve the aircraft for return to service unless they hold an Inspection Authorization.

2. No. The change is a minor alteration.

3. 48 hours.

CHAPTER 7

1. Owner or operator of the aircraft.

2. Yes.

3. When it has been rebuilt by the manufacturer.

4. The rotor is a life-limited part.

5. So there is a separate record for the propeller if it is transferred to another engine.

6. Total time in service, current status of life-limited parts, and the time since last overhaul of the items required to be overhauled on a time basis, current inspection status of the aircraft, status of applicable airworthiness directives, and a current list of major alterations.

7. Form 337

8. The owner or operator of the aircraft.

9. A minimum of one year unless sooner superceded by other work.

CHAPTER 8

1. Date, description of work or reference to data of the repair, name, signature, and certificate number of the person approving the repair.

2. An authorized representative of the repair station.

3. Date, total time, type of inspection, certification statement, signature, and certificate number of the person approving the inspection.

4. True

5. Yes. A 100-hour inspection can be signed off as unairworthy.

6. Date, total time, AD number, AD amendment number, revision date, method of compliance, next due time or date, name, signature and certificate number of the person performing the AD compliance.

7. Two.

8. One copy is placed in the owner's maintenance record and one copy is sent to the local FAA district office.

CHAPTER 9

1. False. The Airworthiness Certificate should be retained in the aircraft at all times.

2. There is an endorsement page with an FAA official's signature and FAA-approval statement.

3. Consult the aircraft manufacturer.

4. By obtaining a special airworthiness certificate.

5. One flight only.

FINAL EXAMINATION

AIRCRAFT INSPECTION AND MAINTENANCE RECORDS

Select the best, or correct answer from the choices listed below the questions.

1. Who is primarily responsible for maintaining an aircraft in airworthy condition?
   A&P technician
   Owner or operator
   FAA inspector
   Authorized Inspector

2. On aircraft requiring an annual inspection how often is this inspection required?
   A. Once a year
   B. 12 months
   C. 24 months
   D. 12 calendar months

3. How many hours may a 100-hour inspection be exceeded by if necessary to fly to a place where the inspection can be performed?
   A. 1 hour
   B. 5 hours
   C. 10 hours
   D. 20 hours

4. If an annual inspection is completed on June 6, 2005, when will the inspection period expire?
   A. June 6, 2006
   B. June 1, 2006
   C. June 30, 2005
   D. June 30, 2006

5. Who can perform and approve for return to service an annual inspection?
   A. A&P with Inspection Authorization
   B. A&P technician
   C. Owner or operator
   D. Repair Station

6. Who can approve an aircraft for return to service after a 100-hour inspection has been completed?
   A. Repair station
   B. A&P technician
   C. Owner or operator
   D. Repairman

7. What is required to fly an aircraft after the annual inspection has expired to a place where it can be performed?
   A. Nothing is needed as it can be exceeded by 5 hours.
   B. Owner's permission
   C. An A&P technician's permission
   D. A special flight or ferry permit from the FAA

8. What type of inspection is required when an aircraft is placed on a progressive inspection program?
   A. Manufacturer's recommended inspection
   B. A phase inspection
   C. Annual inspection
   D. A special FAA inspection

9. Who must supervise a progressive inspection system on an aircraft?
   A. Owner or operator
   B. Authorized inspector
   C. A&P technician
   D. Any repair station

10. Who can sign off or approve for return to service the various phases of a progressive inspection?
    A. A&P technician
    B. Repairman
    C. Any repair station
    D. Owner or operator

11. Who must select the type of inspection program that is used on a large or turbine powered multi-engine aircraft?
    A. Owner or operator
    B. Authorized inspector
    C. National Transportation Safety Board
    D. FAA

12. What is issued by the FAA to correct unsafe conditions that may exist in an aircraft?
    A. Service Bulletins
    B. Airworthiness Directives
    C. Service Letters
    D. Technical Standard Orders

13. A manufacturer of an aircraft may issue information concerning an improvement or change that may be made on an aircraft, these changes are called:

    A. Airworthiness Directives

    B. Service Bulletins

    C. Technical Standard Orders

    D. Advisory Circulars

14. When inspecting the seat belts in an aircraft what TSO number should be printed on the identification tag?

    A. TSO C14A

    B. TSO C15C

    C. TSO C22B

    D. TSO C64A

15. What aircraft document must be displayed in the interior of the aircraft?

    A. Registration certificate

    B. Airworthiness certificate

    C. FCC license

    D. Weight and balance data

16. What appendix in 14 CFR Part 43 covers the minimum inspection requirements on an aircraft?

    A. Appendix A

    B. Appendix B

    C. Appendix C

    D. Appendix D

17. According to 14 CFR Part 43 what must be used in performing an inspection on an aircraft?

    A. A flashlight

    B. An inspection mirror

    C. A checklist

    D. A magnifying glass

18. On an aircraft equipped with a retractable landing gear what must be done during the inspection to insure proper operation of the landing gear?

    A. Disassemble and overhaul the strut assembly

    B. Change fluid in the strut

    C. Dye check the retraction links

    D. Perform a retraction and extension check

19. When performing a 100-hour inspection on the engine you are required to:

    A. Retorque all the cylinder hold down bolts

    B. Perform a compression check

    C. Grind the valves

    D. Change the spark plugs

20. Before approving an aircraft for returns to service following a 100-hour inspection you are required to:

    A. Operate the engine and perform certain functional checks

    B. Notify the local FAA office

    C. Test fly the aircraft

    D. Taxi the aircraft

21. When inspecting the ELT on an aircraft you should check:

    A. Date of installation

    B. Date of last operational check

    C. Date of battery replacement

    D. Date of TSO compliance

22. When performing the operational check on the engine which of the following RPM checks should be done?

    A. Idle and cruise RPM

    B. Static and cruise RPM

    C. Cruise and full power RPM

    D. Idle and static RPM

23. Who is primarily responsible for having and maintaining the aircraft maintenance records?

    A. A&P technician performing the work on the aircraft

    B. Owner or operator of the aircraft

    C. FAA

    D. An authorized inspector

24. Who is responsible for making appropriate entries in the maintenance records after performing an inspection or maintenance on the aircraft?

    A. A&P technician performing the work on the aircraft

    B. Owner or operator of the aircraft

    C. FAA

    D. Pilot of the aircraft

25. Which of the following is considered to be a part of the permanent maintenance records on an aircraft?

    A. Time in service of the aircraft

    B. Record of all annual inspections

    C. Record of all service bulletins complied with

    D. Record of all 100-hour inspections

26. How long must temporary maintenance records be retained?

    A. 6 months, unless sooner superseded by other work

B. 9 months, unless sooner superseded by other work

C. 12 months, unless sooner superseded by other work

D. 24 months, unless sooner superseded by other work

27. The five items required in a maintenance record entry returning a minor repair to service are:

A. Date, tach time, description of work, signature, and certificate number

B. Date, total time, description of work, name and certificate number

C. Total time, description of work, signature, and certificate number

D. Date, description of work, a name, signature, and certificate number

28. The six items required in a maintenance record entry approving a 100-hour inspection for return to service are:

A. Date, total time, type of inspection, certification statement, signature, and certificate number

B. Date, tach time, certification statement, name, signature, and certificate number

C. Date, total time, tach time, certification statement, name, and certificate number

D. Date, tach time, type of inspection, signature, and certificate number

29. The form used to record and approve for return to service major alterations and repairs is called a Form:

A. 802

B. 727

C. 337

D. 2350

30. The information required in a maintenance record entry for the compliance with a recurring airworthiness directive are:

A. Date, tach time, AD number, signature, and certificate number

B. Date, total time, AD number, revision date, method of compliance, next due time or date, name, signature, and certificate number

C. Date, total time, AD number, method of compliance, signature, certificate number

D. Date, AD number, method of compliance, name, signature, and certificate number

ANSWERS TO FINAL EXAMINATION

AIRCRAFT INSPECTION AND MAINTENANCE RECORDS

1. B
2. D
3. C
4. D
5. A
6. B
7. D
8. C
9. B
10. A
11. A
12. B
13. B
14. C
15. B
16. D
17. C
18. D
19. B
20. A
21. C
22. D
23. B
24. A
25. A
26. C
27. D
28. A
29. C
30. B